LOVE IS STRONGER THAN DEATH

Love Is Stronger Than Death

PETER J. KREEFT

1817

Published in San Francisco by **Harper & Row, Publishers**

NEW YORK, HAGERSTOWN, SAN FRANCISCO, LONDON

Acknowledgment is made for permission to quote from Edna St. Vincent Millay's "Dirge Without Music," from *Collected Poems,* Harper & Row, copyright © 1928, 1955 by Edna St. Vincent Millay and Norma Millay Ellis.

FIRST EDITION

Designed by Jim Mennick

Library of Congress Cataloging in Publication Data

Kreeft, Peter.
  LOVE IS STRONGER THAN DEATH.
  1. Death—Meditations. I. Title.
BT825.K68 1979   128'.5   78–15839
ISBN 0–06–064774–4

---

79 80 81 82 83 10 9 8 7 6 5 4 3 2 1

For my father and my mother,
from whom I learned the
meaning of death and life.

Contents

Dear, beauteous death! the jewel of the just,
  shining nowhere but in the dark;
What mysteries do lie beyond thy dust,
  Could man outlook that mark!

HENRY VAUGHAN (1622–1695),
  *"They Are All Gone into the
  World of Light"*

Foreword

Death is the one implacable topic. We mortals ("mortals"—there it is!) can never stop thinking about it. We can never stop trying to do something about it. Indeed, it seems to have been one of the first things we did try to do something about. Dig as far as we will into archeological mounds in Mesopotamia, Africa, or Sutton Hoo, and we find—what? Burial artifacts. Coffins, spices, food and armor for the soul on its journey, memorial tablets—something, anything, to bring to this impalpable mystery. Ubi sunt? Indeed.

No. I am wrong. We can stop thinking about it. Our own epoch tried it. We spread euphemism over it like treacle. Instead of howling wakes, long palls, drawn hearses, and "Dies Irae," we tried parlors and carpets and slumber rooms and cosmetics and the fetching imagery of Forest Lawn with its nooks and glades and general ambience of baby's-boat's-a-silver-moon. All is well, all is well, if only we don't *look*. (Said in a tone quite different from the Lady Julian, who, having looked quite long and hard, was able to say with towering courage and candor, "All shall be well, and all shall be well." Not the same thing at all.)

But no again. I am not wrong. We can't stop thinking about it. Suddenly (ten years ago?) we decided that, since we are bringing the clipboards and questionnaires of society to every other topic, we may do so with this topic. So we briskly set about approaching the ultimate monster in the same way. Let's see now, let's tabulate the progressive attitudes of the dying person. And let's calculate the responses of those surrounding the situation. And let's enumerate and observe and tally and summarize and generalize. It is *data,* and our specialty now is data. Sex data, marriage data, urban data, data about syndromes and neuroses and hostilities and attitudes and prejudices. If only we can get it all *taped* somehow. . . .

And thus a plethora of books about death. One more topic. How to die.

And all the while the monster is grinning at us, unimpressed, implacable, inexorable, gobbling us up one by one while we whisk at the gnats flying about his serene brow. He is still our enemy.

So says Peter Kreeft. There is no getting around it; there is no point in sentimentalizing it; nothing is to be gained by artful dodges. Death is our enemy, our last enemy. Aha. Bravo to Peter Kreeft for pricking us back toward the sheer lucidity with which our ancestors looked at death.

And then what? Death is a stranger, he says. Yes, fair enough. It certainly is. So far so good. But what's this? Death as a friend? Wait, are we being wheedled into yet another mire of sentiment? Will we find the abyss once more papered over with febrile attempts to make death "natural" and therefore unterrifying and welcome?

Oh, oh, worse and worse. Death as mother. And, final, frantic outrage, death as lover. Well, we can set this book aside as one more attempt (albeit an enormously keen and ingenious attempt) to tiptoe past the intractable.

No. I am wrong indeed this time. This book prods and huddles us along a track right down into and through the dark mystery of death, never winking, never dodging, never flinching, never bidding us avert our eyes. We are driven (that is the word, I think—Peter Kreeft will not allow us to loiter timorously in byways where we might be pleased to find false shelter), driven much farther into the topic than the "books-about-death" have dared take us. Follow Peter Kreeft in this journey into the abyss and find out how to begin thinking about it with a candor born of true radicalism, that is, the effort to get to the root— the *radix*—of a question.

Death as friend? As mother? As lover? How can we say that without the most insufferable sentimentalism?

Read this and find out.

THOMAS HOWARD

Hamilton, Mass.
Epiphany 1978

Introduction

I am writing this book about death for an intensely personal reason. I have a terminal illness.

You are invited to read it for the same reason. You too have a terminal illness.

We are never mistaken in our prognosis of this illness: Life is always fatal. No one gets out of it alive. "As doctors, when they examine the state of a patient and recognize that death is at hand, pronounce: 'He is dying, he will not recover,' so we must say from the moment a man is born: 'He will not recover.' "[1]

I invite you to a journey of exploration with me into the land of death, "the undiscovered country from whose bourn no traveller returns."[2] We live in this country, and we should know the country we live in. We should discover "the undiscovered country."

It is a mysterious country, an impenetrable jungle, a bottomless pit. The questions What is death? and Why do we die? are the deepest of all questions. They are questions the poet, the philosopher, the mystic, and the child ask; and they are questions the poet, philosopher, mystic, and child in each of us asks. We keep asking. We obviously have not yet finished answering. Death still smiles sphinxlike at us. We have not unravelled her riddle. There is little danger that this book will. Its purpose is to stimulate exploration, not to end it. Perhaps the only thing that is clear about death is that we cannot be clear about it. Perhaps the only wisdom we can have about death is Socrates's wisdom, the knowledge of our own ignorance. That is at least where we have to start.

> ZORBA THE GREEK: Why do the young die? Why does anybody die, tell me?
> SCHOLAR: I don't know.
> ZORBA: What's the use of all your damn books? If they don't tell you that, what the hell do they tell you?
> SCHOLAR: They tell me about the agony of men who can't answer questions like yours.[3]

The question of the meaning of death is also the question of the meaning of life, the greatest of all questions. Death puts life into question. Don Quixote is talking about this when he tells Sancho Panza about the look he saw in the eyes of the soldiers who lay dying in his arms; the eyes seemed to be asking a question. Sancho asks, "Was it the question 'Why am I dying?'" and Quixote replies, "No, it was the question 'Why was I living?'"

Because of death, the question of the meaning of life leads to one of two answers. Because death exists, because life ends in death, because the final fact about life is death, life is either startlingly more meaningful or startlingly less meaningful than we usually think. For if even death is meaningful, then life is startlingly more meaning-full; than we usually think; and if death is not meaningful, then life, in the final analysis, is not meaning-full. For death is the final analysis. If there is nothing at the end of the road, then the road leads nowhere, points to nothing, means nothing. No compromise is possible on this, the ultimate question: Is life as a whole, life in the long run, meaningful or meaningless? Life cannot be meaningful in the short run and meaningless in the long run, because the long run is the meaning of the short run. "One foot up and one foot down/ That's the way to London town"—if there is no London, or if it's not worth going to, then there's no reason to put one foot up and one foot down.

So life is either totally meaningful or totally meaningless, depending on what death is. Therefore we had better try to find out what death is.

ABOUT THIS BOOK

This is a philosophy of death. Much has been written lately on the medical and psychological aspects of death, and on the cultural and sociological aspects of death; but the primary question is surely the philosophical one, What *is* death? How we approach death, feel about death, cope with death, and actually die depends on what death *is*. What is its essence, its meaning? That is what we explore in this book. It is about death, not just about attitudes towards death. It asks first-order questions, not second-order questions—questions about reality, not questions about questions, views, opinions, or attitudes.

Its goal is not to be current, challenging, clever, comprehensive, contemporary, complete, or comforting—only true. I write today about death not because it is a timely topic but because it is a timeless topic. What is timeless is always timely. The "spirit of the times" is soon dated; what is most up to date is most quickly out of date, like a date itself. I seek, like Thoreau, to "read not the *Times;* read the eternities." If this sounds snobbish, it shouldn't; it is the opposite of snobbery. The merely avant-garde thinker is the real snob. The object of his snobbery is not the living but the dead, the great "silent majority" of precontemporary thinkers who are disenfranchised not by accident of birth but by accident of death. I want to extend the franchise; I want to practice what Chesterton called "the democracy of the dead." For most of what I have learned about death I have learned from the dead. From one in particular, C. S. Lewis, I have learned (among many other things) how to learn from the dead. Lewis did for me what he said Owen Barfield did for him:

> made short work of ..."chronological snobbery," the uncritical assumption
> whatever has gone out of date is on that account discredited.[4]

One last point: this book is condensed. When I read the average three-hundred-page book, I wish the author had condensed it to one hundred pages. Words and time are two of our most precious commodities. I shall try to use both sparingly. Such a book should be read in a special way: slowly and thoughtfully. "Some books are to be tasted, others are to be swallowed, still others are to be chewed and digested."[5] Don't rush; relish, savor, pause, explore, poke around. Enjoy.

THREE QUESTIONS: DEATH, LIFE AND GOD

What is death? Everyone would agree with this definition: death is the end of life. But "end" can mean two very different things. The end of a baseball game is when the last out has been made; also, the end of a baseball game is to score the most runs. The end of the class is when the dismissal bell rings; also, the end of the class is to learn. The end of sculpting is when the last stroke of the hammer has been made; also, the end of sculpting is to create a piece of sculpture. The end of loving is when lovers cease to love; also, the end of loving is for lovers to perfect their love. The first sense of "end" is finish, cessation, termination; the second is purpose, point, goal, or consummation. Now: Is death the end of life? Yes, the termination of life is death. But is death also the goal and consummation of life? It would seem very strange to say so. Death removes life, and the removal of a thing is not its consummation. How could ceasing to live be the consummation and purpose of living?

But if death is not the end of life in this sense of "end," why do we die? And how is death related to the end of life? Clearly we cannot answer these questions unless we know what *is* the end of life. We do not know why we die unless we know why we live.

Talk about the end or meaning of life raises the question of God. For if there is a God, God is the meaning of life. There may be *gods* that are not the meaning of our life; there may be higher species of life that have their own separate destinies and businesses: spirits, angels, extraterrestrial life forms, and so on. These would be ingredients in the universe, But if there is a God, God is not an ingredient in the universe, not a finite part of the whole show—but the point of it all. That is simply the meaning of the word *God*.

But is there such a God? And who or what might God be? Talk about God today runs the risk of talking about nothing, that is, nothing in the experience of the listener. Perhaps God is not dead, but the *word* 'God' often seems to be.

Talk about God is not talk about anything in many people's experience today. It is certainly not talk about anything in empirical experience—in *anyone*'s empirical experience in any day. But death is an empirical experience, and the question of a life after death *is* a question about empirical experience—in fact, about the postmortem empirical experience of everyone, in every day. Death makes the question of God an empirically testable question. Death makes the abstract God-question concrete. Instead of "Is there a God?" the question becomes "Will I see God?" It is a dramatic thought, the thought of meeting God at death. Death gives life to the God-question. Perhaps we shall find death giving life to many other things too.

We have lost all our absolutes today except one. Once, we had God, truth, morality, family, fidelity, work, country, common sense, and many others—perhaps too many others. Now, in the age of absolute relativism, one absolute is left: death. Death is the one pathway through which all people at all times raise the question of the absolute, the question of God. The last excuse for not raising the God-question is Thoreau's "one world at a time."[6] Death removes this last excuse.

We have seen three questions intertwining, leading to and from each other, like magnetic paths. However they twist and turn into the darkness, they stay close to each other and intersect again and again. The three questions are Death and Life and God. This journey of exploration will travel all three roads. There is no guarantee at the beginning where they will lead. Will you dare to travel with me on these terrible and wonderful roads? There is no greater journey.

NOTES

1. Augustine *City of God* bk. 3, ch. 10.
2. Shakespeare, *Hamlet,* act 3, scene 1, lines 79–80. Cf. C. S. Lewis, "Hamlet: the Prince or the Poem?" in *Selected Literary Essays* (Cambridge: Cambridge University Press, 1969), pp. 88–105 for a refreshingly different approach to the play, one that resolves many of the traditional critical disagreements about the character, motivation, and procrastination of the protagonist by seeing the play's center as death, not Hamlet's psyche.
3. Nikos Kazantzakis, *Zorba the Greek,* trans. Carl Wildman (New York: Simon & Schuster, 1952).
4. C. S. Lewis, *Surprised by Joy* (New York: Harcourt, Brace and World, 1955), pp. 207–208.
5. Francis Bacon, "Of Studies," in *Essays* (British Book Center, 1974).
6. Henry David Thoreau (according to the account of Parker Pillsbury, an intimate friend of the Thoreau family). Cited in F. B. Sanborn, *The Personality of Thoreau* (Folcroft, Pa.: The Folcroft Press, 1901), p. 69: "Then I spoke only once more to him. . . . I think my question was substantially this: 'You seem so near the brink of the dark river, that I almost wonder how the opposite shore may appear to you.' He then answered: 'One world at a time.' "

CHAPTER 1

Death as an Enemy

At every stage of our journey we meet death, the same death. But death is not the same to us at every stage of our journey. Death wears many faces. What death *is* behind all the faces it wears, we may never know; or we may know only after we have seen all its faces and then looked behind them. We shall know only at the end of our journey, if at all, who or what it is that wears the faces.

There is a progression to our journey. Death wears five faces, and the only way to see each of them is to have seen others first. Each face is a password to the next—the first face is a password to the second, the second to the third, and so on. The password to the first face of death is simply life, being alive. It is a password each of us can speak.

DEATH IS AN ENEMY

The first face of death is that of an enemy. If death does not first appear to us as an enemy, then it cannot appear truly as a friend, or as anything greater than a friend. Death cannot immediately appear as a friend. Death cannot *be* a friend; it can only *become* a friend, after first being an enemy. Otherwise, it is not death that is a friend, but something else that we confuse with death, such as sleep, or rest, or peace.

Many currently popular books on death teach this confusion. They tell us to accept death as natural. They claim thus to break the spell of "the American way of death." that is, denying and ignoring death, treating it as a stranger. The claim is false. What this teaching really does is add to the denial of death, the ignoring of death. For what death *is,* first of all, is our enemy. To see more than this is one thing; to see less is quite another. It is like the difference between toleration and forgiveness. Forgiveness sees more than evil, toleration sees less. Forgiveness faces evil, admits it, and sees beyond it, forgiving it. Mere toleration refuses to face or admit evil; it says, "There's nothing to forgive." Instead of freeing from evil, toleration blocks the way to that freedom. In the same way, accepting death as natural does not give us "freedom-towards-death"[1] but blocks the way to that freedom. It fails to see death as an enemy; and even if it truly causes us to see death as a friend instead of ignoring it or treating it as a stranger, the idea is premature. Like a radically premature baby, its life expectancy is not great. It is an answer without a question; it comes too soon. It is like an ideological indoctrination given to a docile, unquestioning child. It is like the wise man who ran joyously into the street, shouting: "I've found the answer! I've found the answer!"—then stopped, confused—he had forgotten the question. Perhaps the acceptance of death as a friend is the answer (or at least *an* answer), but death as an enemy is the question.

A *New York Times* book reviewer commented on the current rash of books "explaining" death to children as natural and therefore to be accepted.

> All of these stories were written with a didactic purpose: to give a child a way of looking at death and living with the knowledge of it. All of them try to diffuse the finality, the fearfulness, by presenting death as just another natural process. But to most adults in our culture, death is more than just another natural process. It is an occasion surrounded with mystery and deep emotions. Presenting it to a child as just another change we go through is less than candid.[2]

Such books seek to take from the child only the fear of death. But they take from him instead something of great value, our culture's last absolute, its last mystery, and its last transcendence.

A few years ago, a relative of my neighbor died suddenly and unexpectedly at the age of three. My neighbor's son, then about seven, asked his mother, "Where is my cousin now?" She did not believe in any form of life after death and she wanted to be honest with her son, so she could not tell him that his cousin was now in Heaven. But she had just read one of the books I have criticized on how to talk to children about death, and its 'wisdom' made sense to her—but not to her son. She answered, "Your cousin has gone back to the earth, where we all came from. All of nature is a cycle. Death is a natural part of that cycle. When you see the earth put forth new flowers next spring, you can know that your cousin's life is fertilizing those flowers." She was so naïve that she was surprised when her son screamed, "I don't want him to be fertilizer!" and ran off.

The old myths are wiser than the new demythologized books. They grow from our race's subconsious and embody its intuitive wisdom. It is a remarkable fact that all the myths throughout the world see death not as natural but as unnatural, as an accident, a fall, a mistake, a catastrophe that could have been averted but wasn't. The myth of paradise lost is universal, appearing in many forms: Adam eats forbidden fruit; Pandora opens a box; a bird drops the magic berry of immortality; Primal Woman throws a stone at the sky and chases the gods away.[3] Only then does death appear. Why do all the variations insist on this single theme of paradise lost, of death as an accident? Because death does not *feel* natural, however biologically necessary it may be. This feeling about death cannot be put to death by reasonable considerations about the cycles of nature. Man does not *feel* like recycled fertilizer.

Though Freud is the champion of feeling, he is by no means the champion of myth but of reason and science. That is why he teaches that we must "make friends with the necessity of dying."[4] This is the perfectly reasonable but inhuman philosophy of Stoicism, of resignation to fate, to the inevitable. It is not courage, as it claims to be; it is cowardice. Must we accept brute force? Must we make friends with our enemy simply because he is stronger? That is the philosophy of the Quisling, the attitude that endures tyrants. Death seeks to be a tyrant. Death *is* stronger. It always wins. Our choice is between fighting on the good but losing side, or fighting on the evil, winning side. If we have courage, we will go down with the ship because it is the good ship, the human ship, H.M.S. Life. But if we are cowards, we will jump ship, or parley with our enemy. It is not courage to "make friends with the necessity of dying"; it is courage to say "Do not go gentle into that good night./ Rage, rage against the dying of the light."[5] *That* is honesty. It is calling light light and darkness darkness. "Woe unto them that call evil good, and good evil; that put darkness for light, and light for darkness; that put bitter for sweet, and sweet for bitter."[6]

Like Isaiah the prophet, Norse mythology can also teach us that honesty and that courage. In it even the gods will be defeated and Asgard destroyed. Should we therefore accept the conqueror, the enemy? No! One meaningful choice remains: to be a man to the last, to fight on the side of men and gods—and life—even if it is the losing side. To worship goodness, not power; life, not success; the right, not the inevitable.

We know death is inevitable. We know death will win. But to know is not to accept.

> Down, down, down into the darkness of the grave
> Gently they go, the beautiful, the tender, the kind;
> Quietly they go, the intelligent, the witty, the brave.
> I know. But I do not approve. And I am not resigned.[7]

DEATH IS LOSS

Death is loss, loss of life. Life is good. Loss of a good is an evil. Therefore death is an evil. Loss of a great good is a great evil. Life is a great good. Therefore death is a great evil. Not to see this is a great blindness. Blindness is a great evil. Therefore not to see death as a great evil is a great evil.

Death is loss of being, denial of being, the enemy of being. It is the reduction of being to nonbeing, the undoing of creation. Death is the most uncreative thing there is. It literally uncreates creation, whether it is the creation of man or God, whether it is a painting destroyed by fire, or a nation destroyed by war, a soul destroyed by vice, or a body destroyed by cancer. Death is the enemy of God. It undoes the divine work, creation. If man is the friend of God, he must be the enemy of death. God's enemy must be his enemy. "Do I not hate them that hate Thee, O God? I hate them with perfect hatred; I count them my enemies."[8]

DEATH IS NOT SLEEP

Death is not sleep. We live through sleep unchanged, but even if we live through death, we do not live through it unchanged. If we awaken from death, we do not awaken to our old self and world. They are gone forever—extinct. "I look up at the night sky. Is there anything more certain than that in all those vast times and spaces, were I allowed to search them, I should never again find her voice, her face? She died. She is dead. Is the word so hard to learn?"[9]

We like to think of death as a sleep. It comforts us. But it is a lie. Sleep is relaxation, rest for the weary. Death appears as the opposite: extreme rigor *(rigor mortis)*, like one entering some great trial. From this side of death, the body of death is hard and silent, an enormous nothing, a hole.

THE APPEARANCE OF DEATH VS. THE REALITY OF DEATH

This is how death appears. The reality of death *may* be more than the appearance of death. The distinction between appearance and reality is one of the most important distinctions the human mind has ever discovered. It is the origin of philosophy and of science, and probably of every kind of questioning. For if appearances are accepted as equal to reality, we do not question them to uncover any further, unknown, hidden reality behind them.

Perhaps death conceals a great secret behind its appearances, like the human face, like the face of nature, and like the faces of the gods in mythology. Perhaps Death has two sides, two faces: a manifest face and a hidden face. Its manifest face looks like a hole, a bottomless pit. Perhaps its hidden face is a door. If so, we must first explore the hole to find the door. The door is *in* the hole. The hidden face is under the mask. We must look further into the mask, the mask that says "I am your enemy."

DEATH IS LOSS OF LIGHT

The mask, the face of death presented to us in all the many myths of humanity, is remarkably uniform. In the first place, death is always seen as a place down, under or in the earth, in contrast with the sky, wherein dwell the immortals, the gods. It is a place of darkness, not light. Dead bodies belong in a grave, a dark hole in the earth. The earth is the place of death. In the second place, not only does death have a place, death also has a time. Just as death's place is down, not up, so death's time is the past, not the future. Death is the end of our futures. It is like undoing birth and life and growth and newness. It is as if we strive *ahead* only to be dragged *back* to the nothingness that preceded our birth, just as we struggle *upward* to the light only to be dragged back *down* to the darkness of the grave.

That is why death is often seen as sleep. It is not sleep, but it is like sleep. It appears as a loss of alertness, awakedness, aliveness, awareness; a loss of enlightenment. Buddha calls himself The Enlightened One, "the man who woke up" (that is what the title 'Buddha' means), implying that the rest of us are dreaming. Socrates sees himself as an intellectual midwife, helping our ideas be born into the light of day, implying that we are sleeping. Jesus, even more radically, preaches the necessity of being "born again," assuming that we are not only sleeping but dead! Being born, waking up—this is life. Sleeping, in the womb or in the dream—this is death. The poets have always known that the tomb, the womb, and the dream are somehow one.

We want to wake up. Sleep, dream—this is our enemy. Truth, awakening, enlightenment—this is our friend. Therefore, even if death *is* a sleep, death is our enemy.

Death is the enemy of everything good: life, growth, awakening, enlightenment, creation, being. The more we love these goods, the more we will refuse to make peace with their enemy. The more you love your brother, the more you hate the cancer that is destroying him. The more you love life, the more you refuse to accept death. No one with honesty and blood, no one who loves life with courage and passion, no one who is loyal to life, can simply "accept death."

The "accept death" literature tries to combat our society's avoidance of death. This is good. But it has the wrong motive. The same motive that led our society to avoid death now leads to its acceptance, namely, the avoidance of pain and tragedy and unanswerable questions, the demand for comfort and security. The means for gaining these ends is changed; we accept death instead of avoiding it. But the ends themselves are the same—homeostasis, adjustment, resolution, peace.

Our end in this exploration is not peace or comfort. It is truth. Truth is not comfortable, but it is life, not death. It is awakening, not dreaming. For the love of life, let us pursue the truth about death.

DEATH AS INEVITABLE

St. Augustine, in one of his sermons,[10] says something like this: Listen to people speculating about a newborn baby. Listen to what they say. Will he live to a ripe old age? Perhaps so, perhaps not. Will he do some great deed? Perhaps so, perhaps not. Will he marry and have children? Perhaps so, perhaps not. Will his life be happy? Perhaps so, perhaps not. Will he be a good man? Perhaps so, perhaps not. Why does no one say Will he die? Perhaps so, perhaps not?

It is not true that death and taxes are the only two certainties. Taxes are not certain.

We find ourselves plunged at birth into a madly rushing river that emerges from a dark subterranean cavern. The river rushes always in one direction—down, toward another subterranean cavern, equally dark, equally unexplorable. And into that cave of death the river of life disappears forever. Between two empty and silent infinities we "strut and fret our hour upon the stage."[11]

The Venerable Bede, in his *Ecclesiastical History,* tells the story of Paulinus, a Christian missionary who came to the English kingdom of Northumbria in 627 A.D. The king held council with his advisers to decide whether to welcome the new religion or not. Finally a wise old thane arose and gave this advice:

> Your Majesty, when we compare the present life of man with that time of which we have no knowledge, it seems to me like the swift flight of a lone sparrow through the banqueting-hall where you sit in the winter months to dine with your thanes and counsellors. Inside there is a comforting fire to warm the room; outside, the wintry storms of snow and rain are raging. This sparrow flies swiftly in through one door of the hall, and out through another. While he is inside, he is safe from the winter storms; but after a few moments of comfort, he vanishes from sight into the darkness whence he came. Similarly, man appears on earth for a little while, but we know nothing of what went before this life, and what follows. Therefore if this new teaching can reveal any more certain knowledge, it seems only right that we should follow it.[12]

Or, to change the image, we find ourselves locked in a car plunging at breakneck speed down an immense hill toward the edge of a cliff, with the brakes useless and the steering locked.[13] At birth we find ourselves at the top of the hill, coming from nowhere. We fall always in one direction. The hill is time, and life; and we always end by falling over the edge into the abyss.

Nothing avails against this abyss. Whether or not we rage against the night, the night falls. History and literature abound with testimonies to this terrible truth. A fool saw Solon the Greek sage weeping for the death of his son and offered him the cold comfort of reason: "Why do you weep, since weeping avails nothing?" Wise Solon replied, "Precisely because it avails nothing."

DEATH AS IRREVERSIBLE

Death is irreversible. "We must all die; we are like water spilt on the ground, which cannot be gathered up again."[14] As Job says:

> There is always hope for a tree:
>   when felled, it can start its life again;
>   its shoots continue to sprout.
> Its roots may be decayed in the earth,
>   its stump withering in the soil,
> but let it scent the water, and it buds,
>   and puts out branches like a plant new set.
> But man? He dies, and lifeless he remains;
>   man breathes his last, and then where is he?
> The waters of the seas may disappear,
>   all the rivers may run dry or drain away;
> but man, once in his resting place, will never rise again.
>   The heavens will wear away before he wakes,
>   before he rises from his sleep.[15]

Death is irreversible because time is irreversible. Because time is irreversible, every act in time is irreversible. What's done cannot be undone. Even if I undo the consequences of an act, I cannot undo having done it. The prodigal returned home is now the *prodigal* returned home. Even if his home is the same, he is not. That's why "you can't go home again." A divorcee is not a virgin.

Since death is in time, death is irreversible. Even if there is life after death, death is irreversible.

In fact, time is another word for death. Time makes every act a little death—at the moment of its being born, the act in time dies forever by becoming part of the past, the dead past, the unchangeable, irreversible, closed past. Today, the now, the only time that is alive, is open and free. But it is dying. In fact, it is dead. It dies at the exact moment of its birth. The only living time—the present—has no time to live between its birth and its death. Time is birth-and-death. Buddha saw this, and called time and all events in time *samsara*, "birth-and-death."

Time the river is fickle and unreliable. Everything it brings us, it steals from us. "Whatever is an arising thing, that also is a ceasing thing," said Buddha, and called this "the pure and spotless eye of the doctrine" of *samsara*.[16] Persons, things, experiences, relationships, civilizations—all the things borne upon us by the river of time are borne away, a world sliding down and away every second into the darkness, never to return. Yeats tells of a little girl on a Normandy beach facing the sea and singing of the many great civilizations that had come and gone in that historic place; she ended each verse with the refrain: "O Lord, let something remain."[17]

Nothing remains.

We are floating in a medium of vast extent, always drifting uncertainly, blown to and fro; whenever we think we have a fixed point to which we can cling and make fast, it shifts and leaves us behind; if we follow it, it eludes our grasp, slips away, and flees eternally before us. Nothing stands still for us. This is our natural state and yet the state most contrary to our inclinations. We burn with desire to find a firm footing, an ultimate, lasting base on which to build a tower rising up to infinity. But our whole foundation cracks and the earth opens up into the depth of the abyss.[18]

All our Towers of Babel come tumbling down, like Humpty-Dumpty.

"You never step into the same river twice," said Heraclitus, "for other and yet other waters are ever flowing on." To which his disciple Cratylus added, "You can't even step into the same river once!"[19] The river, great symbol of life, is also the great symbol of death, for it is the symbol of *samsara,* of time. This river drowns every present in pastness, every life in death, every memory in forgetfulness. The Greeks were shrewd to portray death as the river Lethe, the river of forgetfulness. Memory is our dike against that river, our attempt to stabilize and eternalize time, to "redeem the time" from death. But the dike never holds for long, and the river always wins.

Rivers are irreversible. Clocks are reversible. "You can't go home again" does not mean that you can't turn the clock back (because you can) but that you can't turn the river back. This is true not only of our last exit from home, our final death, but also of a thousand little deaths before it. To be born, we must die to the womb, never to return. To be weaned, we must die to the breast, never to return (though we seek a thousand substitutes). To go to school, we must die to the all-embracing security of the home. To raise a family, we must die to the centrality of the family we came from. To move to a new home, a new job, or a new city, we must die to our old ones. And when we are old and death carries away our relatives, family, and friends, nothing replaces them sometimes except our own loneliness. The supremely lonely act is to die. When we die, we consummate the secret loneliness we inherited at birth. We part from everything—gradually in life, finally in death. All living is parting; all living is dying.

But doesn't life seem to be meetings as well as partings? And may not the last act follow the same script? Our little partings lead to new little meetings; may not our great parting lead to a great meeting? At this point in our journey we have not explored death deeply enough to know. But even if death, like our other partings, leads to something else, and even if that something else is a gain, it is also a loss. A price is paid, the greatest conceivable price: the whole world. Even if it profits a man to lose the whole world to gain his own soul, he must lose the whole world.

And we do not *see* the gain, if there is one. We do not see beyond the walls of the world. At this point in our journey we can only say with Ecclesiastes, "Who knows whether the spirit of man goes upward and the spirit of the beast goes down to the earth?"[20] All we see here "under the sun" is that "a living dog is better than a dead lion."[21]

Alexander the Great had himself buried in a coffin with his hand hanging out, open. He left the world as he entered it, with nothing, testifying to Job's truth: "Naked I came from my mother's womb, and naked I shall return."[22]

DESPAIR

What hope can there be if death is irreversible? If individuals, civilizations, worlds, and galaxies are all born only to die, "what does man gain by all the toil at which he toils under the sun?"[23] "The last act is always tragic, however happy the rest of the play. At the end, a little dirt is shovelled on our head, and that is the end. . . . the end which awaits the noblest life in the world."[24]

> How to keep—is there any, any, is there none such,
>   nowhere known, some bow or brooch or braid or
>   brace, lace, latch or catch or key to keep
> Back beauty, keep it, beauty, beauty, beauty . . .
>   from vanishing away?

Oh, is there no frowning of these wrinkles, rankled
    wrinkles deep,
Down? no waving-off of these most mournful messengers,
    still messengers, sad and stealing messengers of
    gray?
No, there's none, there's none—oh, no, there's none!
Nor can you long be, what you now are, called fair—
Do what you may do, do what you may,
And wisdom is early to despair:
Be beginning; since, no, nothing can be done
To keep at bay
Age and age's evils—hoar hair,
Ruck and wrinkle, drooping, dying, death's worst,
    winding sheets, tombs and worms, and tumbling to
    decay;
So be beginning, be beginning to despair.
Oh, there's none—no, no, no, there's none:
    Be beginning to despair, to despair,
    Despair, despair, despair, despair.[25]

A PUZZLE: THE HEART

But wait. "Spare." There is a puzzle here. We are shocked at the
irreversibility of death although it is utterly familiar, utterly universal,
utterly natural. We find the natural unnatural. Why? Let us be
shocked at our shock. It is shocking that we are shocked at the
inevitable, the familiar, the expected. "This is our natural state and yet
the state most contrary to our inclinations."[26] If the state is not a
puzzle, our inclinations are. "He has made everything beautiful in its
time, and he has put eternity into our hearts,"[27] our desires. If time and
death are not the puzzle, then our hearts are. Our hearts are darker
than death, a greater puzzle than death. Let us explore this even
greater darkness.

    Death is natural; we find it unnatural. Let's look at both halves of
the puzzle. First, death's naturalness. Death is essential to nature; it is
death that allows everything in nature to live. We live by eating dead
animals and plants; animals live by eating dead plants. New people,
animals, and plants come to live to replace old ones that die. Death is
the fertilizer to life. We know this. "Did so-and-so die? Ah, well, that's
life!"

Yet we rebel. Death is as natural as the world, but we rebel against the world, we have a lover's quarrel with the world.

If you are really a product of a materialistic universe, how is it you don't feel at home there? Do fish complain of the sea for being wet? Or if they did, would that fact itself not strongly suggest that they had not always been, or would not always be, purely aquatic creatures? Notice how we are perpetually *surprised* at Time. ('How time flies! Fancy John being grown-up and married! I can hardly believe it!') In heaven's name, why? Unless, indeed, there is something in us which is *not* temporal.[28]

What is this something?

In the name of what do we quarrel? What do we want? We hardly know. "Thou has put eternity in his heart"—what is eternity? We don't really know, but we do know that our heart wants something more than death and time and the world of endlessly repeated cycles. We may not know what eternity is, but we know what it isn't. That's what keeps us asking "Is that all there is?" even after repeated experience, time after tiresome time, assures us that it is. It is as if a little bird in us continues to be fed new varieties of food—cat food, dog food, people food—and keeps asking: "Is that all there is?" None of it seems to be bird food. It is as if a child is given a thousand Christmas presents and keeps asking after each one? "Is that all there is?" Either the child is very greedy and ungrateful, or else someone has made him a promise and not yet kept it—promised him a pet, perhaps, but so far given him only a thousand inanimate toys.

What *do* we want? In the name of what do we ask "Is that all there is?" Certainly not mere survival after death, not merely more of the same, ten more years or ten million. That would be just more dog food, more toys. What do we want? Why do we see death as the face of an enemy? The two questions are one.

Here is a clue we must follow, an avenue to explore, a possible hope at the center of our despair at death. We are shocked at death, we find the natural unnatural. Why?

FOLLOWING UP THE CLUE: DEATH AS EXCEPTIONAL

Perhaps we are shocked at death because of its finality. Nothing in nature is final. Everything changes, recurs, comes back in cycles. We see no absolute in nature except one, our death. If nothing in nature is final and death is final, it logically follows that death is not something in nature, or at least not only something in Nature. If nothing in nature is absolute and death is absolute, then death is not in nature, not natural. Perhaps that is why it shocks us.

Another's death appears to us as part of nature's relative and changing cycle. Another's death removes only one relative ingredient from our whole world. But our own death is absolute; it removes our whole world. We and our world recover from another's death, but not from our own.

We are shocked at our own death, then, because it is unlike anything else in our experience. It is absolute. Other changes are changes from something to something else, but our death is, for us, the change from something to nothing. Our birth is absolute too—a change from nothing to something—but we do not normally experience that. Our conscious memory does not extend backwards to our birth, but our conscious anticipation does extend forward to our death, so that death does appear even now in our conscious experience through anticipation, and it appears as exceptional. Let us follow the clue of its exceptionalness.

In science, it is always the apparent exception that is the important phenomenon because it is the clue to a deeper or more universal truth hitherto unknown. For instance, radioactivity in that apparently exceptional element radium was the key to the discovery of radioactivity in other elements, and a key to modern nuclear physics. Exceptional civilizations like Greece and Israel are the keys to our history. Exceptional individuals like Socrates and Jesus and Buddha—and Hitler—are our most important clues to the nature of all men, to the unknown Christ within our neighbor or to the "Hitler in ourselves." [29]

There are three puzzles in this exception. First, although we never win, we fight. Although death is inevitable and irreversible, we still rebel. Second, our own death is the only absolute, it seems, in a world of relativities, the only absolutely final event in a world of cycles, the only natural phenomenon that is not natural. The third puzzle is darker still. We have been like spelunkers, explorers of the caves of death; and here is the third cave, hidden under the others, darkest and deepest of all. This puzzle is that death seems to have something to do with guilt. Myths, dreams, and psychoanalysis often reveal a deep feeling of guilt about death. What could this possibly mean?

DEATH AND GUILT

The two most universal taboos concern death and sex. These two most natural things in the world are also the two great mysteries, which we surround with ceremony and myth. Parricide and incest, the two universal taboos, both involve breaking the parental relationship. Our own death too involves breaking a relationship, all relationships. Death is not only a private biological event but the breaking of communion, of all communions, even with Mother Earth and Father Heaven.

Perhaps this is a clue to our clue, an entry into our cave. There is another word, a word which is correlative to guilt, which means the breaking of communion, the severing of relationship. The word is *sin*. Derived from the German *Sünde*, the noun form of *sondern* ("to sunder or cut asunder"), "sin" means first the breaking of a relationship with God. The primary meaning of sin is not breaking divine law but breaking divine love, divine fidelity, divine relationship. Lawbreaking is a secondary, derived meaning. Sinful behavior is derived from a sinful state of being, a state of alienation from God.

A THOUGHT EXPERIMENT

To investigate this cave, let us make an experimental map, a thought experiment. Let us suppose there is a God. And let us suppose that the myths are right: that death came into the world as a consequence of sin—not as an arbitrary and unnecessary punishment inflicted by an angry celestial martinet, but as the inevitable and necessary consequence of sin, as falling is the consequence of jumping off a cliff. To see this, let us suppose that God is the source of all life in the same way that a magnet is the source of magnetism. An iron ring stays magnetized as long as it stays stuck to the magnet, that is, as long as it is not alienated from the magnet. In the same way, a human soul derives life as long as it is not alienated from God. Suppose further that a second iron ring is magnetized as long as it stays stuck to the first. Again, in the same way, the body remains alive as long as it remains with the soul. Suppose too the first ring has free will, and chooses to be its own magnet, its own source of life, and thus separates itself ("sins") from the real magnet (God). The consequences would be, first, that it would fail in its attempt. It does not have within it the source of magnetism, but only a little residual magnetism from the magnet, say, seventy or eighty years of it. Second, the first ring would be able to hold the second ring to it and communicate to it its little residual magnetism only for that short time; once magnetism left it, it would also leave the second ring. In the same way, the death of the body would be a necessary consequence of the death of the soul, which is "sin," or separation from God, the source of life. This explains why Jesus insists that "except a man be born again, he cannot see the Kingdom of God (eternal life)"[30]—birth is the beginning of life. The thought experiment is consistent, and illuminating. Whether or not it is true is another, harder question.

This thought experiment explains why we would feel guilt about death, for it shows the connection between sin and death. We would feel guilt about both these two separations because they fit together as cause and effect, and we brought them both about.

Sometimes we see a direct and individual relation between sin and death. The first death in human history, according to Genesis, was a murder: Cain's murder of his brother Abel. But is not all sin a kind of murder, a desire to kill? For all sin is hate (there are many more kinds of hate than we usually think), and "anyone who hates his brother is a murderer."[31] A Moslem legend tells of a man to whom Allah promised to grant the first two wishes his heart conceived, immediately. As soon as the man looked at his neighbor's house with jealousy, it was destroyed. Then a running child accidentally collided with him and immediately fell dead at his feet. The man then realized to his horror that the wishes of his heart had been granted.

If death is indeed the consequence, symptom, and sign of sin, we are even worse off than we thought. We see in every death not only our defeat but our guilt. This is worse even than defeat. We would rather be killed than killers; or at least we would rather that those we love (our children, for instance) choose to be killed rather than killers if the choice ever came to that. What mother would want her son to collaborate with a cruel and sadistic enemy in war, to torture rather than to be tortured, to murder rather than to be murdered? A live coward may be better than a dead hero, as "a living dog is better than a dead lion," but a live murderer is not better than a dead martyr. We are more terrified by the nightmare of *being* a monster than by the nightmare of being chased by one, because there is no possible escape from the monster we are, but there is one escape from the monster we are not, even if he catches us. The escape is what we are. And now we have discovered (in our thought experiment) that we are monsters, killers, murderers, that we are responsible for death. We have come to the deepest and darkest part of the cave. We can descend no lower than this.

HOPE

Yet in the very floor of this cave we see what might be a light. In the center of our deepest despair we can find a possibility of hope. "Ah, I would not lose my blame! In my blame is my hope," says George Mac Donald.[32] What could this mean? Kierkegaard writes a sermon with the strange title "On the Edification Implied in the Thought: That Over Against God We Are Always in the Wrong."[33] What could this mean? In T. S. Eliot's play, *The Cocktail Party*, Celia says,

> "I should really *like* to think there's something wrong with me—Because, if there isn't, then there's something wrong . . . with the world itself—and that's much more frightening!"[34]

What could this mean?

It means that our ultimate hope is not in ourselves, our innocence, our sanity, but in something more than ourselves, in the reality that gives us meaning. Though we are defeated, reality is not. To say that my hope is in my blame, my guilt, my wrongness, my insanity, means that in the great war between me and reality, reality is right and I am wrong. Reality is not guilty or insane; I am. To blame ourselves (as the story of Adam does in Genesis) is to clear reality, being, truth, the cosmos, the gods, or God. *We may yet be reconciled to reality.* It is we who are out of touch with reality; therefore, there is hope. If reality were out of touch, there would be no hope. If truth itself were false, if reality itself were unreal, if goodness itself were evil, if God were really the devil, if life itself were responsible for death—then all hope of meaning would be gone.

There is hope. Life is not responsible for death; death is not "natural."

There is hope. We are guilty of death.

It is only a thought experiment; but it is a possibility, a hope. The clue of that hope, however, can be followed further only if we do not succumb to the temptation to treat death as a stranger, to ignore death. That is a temptation because once death appears as an enemy, especially an enemy with an accusing face, pointing the finger of guilt at us, the simplest way to deal with it is to ignore it. We do have power over appearances, over what appears to our consciousness, though not over reality. This is the easiest and most popular way of dealing with death.

> Despite his afflictions, man wants to be happy, only wants to be happy, and cannot help wanting to be happy. But how shall he go about it? The best thing would be to make himself immortal; but as he cannot do that, he has decided to stop himself thinking about it.[35]

Thus we turn the enemy into a stranger. "I never knew you, depart from me."[36] If these words were only operative, sacramental, magical words when we spoke them, they would solve the problem of death. But because we have power over appearances, not reality, the words do not banish death but only the appearance of death. Before we try to follow our clue further from despair to hope, we must pause to examine this popular byway, which is really only another form of despair: running from the truth of death. It does not succeed in avoiding death, only in avoiding truth.

NOTES

1. Martin Heidegger, *Being and Time* (New York: Harper & Row, 1962), pp. 264, 266, 384f.
2. Sheila Cole in the *New York Times Book Review,* September 26, 1971, p. 12.
3. Cf. Osborn Segerberg, Jr., *The Immortality Factor* (New York: Dutton, 1974), pp. 9–13.
4. Sigmund Freud, "The Theme of the Three Caskets," in *Character and Culture,* ed. Philip Reiff (New York: Collier Books, 1963), p. 78.
5. Dylan Thomas, "Do Not Go Gentle into That Good Night," in *Collected Poems* (N.Y.: New Directions, 1957).
6. Isa. 5:20 (King James Version).
7. Edna St. Vincent Millay, "Dirge Without Music," in *Collected Poems,* ed. Norma Millay Ellis (New York: Harper & Row, 1956), p. 241.
8. Ps. 139:21, 22. (All Scripture quotations are from the Revised Standard Version unless otherwise noted.)
9. C. S. Lewis, *A Grief Observed* (New York: Seabury Press, 1963), p. 16.
10. Augustine *Sermon* 97. 3.
11. Shakespeare, *Macbeth,* act 5, scene 5, lines 25–26.
12. Beda Venerabilis, *A History of the English Church and People,* trans. Leo Shirley-

Price (Baltimore: Penguin Books, 1955), pp. 124–125.
13. This image is from C. Stephen Evans, *Despair: A Moment or a Way of Life?* (Downers Grove, Ill.: Inter-Versity Press, 1973), p. 10.
14. 2 Sam. 14:14.
15. Job 14:7–12 (Jerusalem Bible).
16. E. A. Burtt, ed., *The Teachings of the Compassionate Buddha* (New York: New American Library Mentor Books, 1955), p. 31.
17. William Butler Yeats, *A Vision* (London, New York: Macmillan, 1937); cf. John S. Dunne, *Time and Myth* (Notre Dame: University of Notre Dame Press, 1975), p. 1.
18. Pascal, *Pensées,* 199 (trans. Krailsheimer). Baltimore: Penguin Books, 1966, p. 92.
19. Heraclitus, Fragment 41–2, in Kathleen Freeman, *The Pre-Socratic Philosophers* (London: Blackwell, 1949). Cf. Francis H. Parker, *The Story of Western Philosophy* (Bloomington, Ind.: Indiana University Press, 1966), pp. 20, 46.
20. Eccles. 3:21.
21. Eccles. 9:4.
22. Job 1:21 (Jerusalem Bible).
23. Eccles. 1:3.
24. Pascal, *Pensées,* 210, 194 (trans. Trotter) New York: E. P. Dutton & Co., 1958, pp. 61, 55.
25. Gerard Manley Hopkins, "The Leaden Echo." in *Poems* ed. W. H. Gardner. London, New York: Oxford University Press, 1948.
26. Pascal, *Pensées,* 199 (trans. Krailsheimer), p. 92.
27. Eccles. 3:11.
28. C. S. Lewis in a letter to Sheldon Vanauken, published in Sheldon Vanauken, *A Severe Mercy* (San Francisco: Harper & Row, 1977), p. 93.
29. Cf. Max Picard, *Hitler in Ourselves,* trans. Heinrich Hauser (Hinsdale, Ill.: Regnery, 1947).
30. John 3:3 (King James Version).
31. 1 John 3:15.
32. C. S. Lewis, *George MacDonald: An Anthology* (New York: Macmillan, 1947), no. 121, p. 61.
33. Søren Kierkegaard, *Either/Or,* vol. 2, (New York: Doubleday Anchor Books, 1959), p. 343.
34. T. S. Eliot, *The Cocktail Party,* act 2 (London: Farber & Farber Ltd., 1974), p. 130.
35. Pascal, *Pensées,* 134 (trans. Krailsheimer), pp. 66–67.
36. Matt. 7:23.

Death as a Stranger

The five faces of death correspond to five human faces, five ways of facing another person, five relationships. Three of the five are forms of love: friendship (Chapter 3), mother-love (Chapter 4), and romantic love (Chapter 5). The other two are the alternatives to love: hate (Chapter 1) and indifference (Chapter 2). Together, these two make up the "fight-or-flight" response (hate being fight and indifference, flight).

HATE VERSUS INDIFFERENCE

The opposite of love is not hate; it is indifference. For we can love and hate the same person at the same time, but we cannot love and be indifferent to the same person at the same time. Hate does not necessarily drive out love, but indifference does.

Love is food. Plants and animals, children and adults all feed and grow on love.* Hate is like poison, but indifference is like starvation.

---

* Anyone can test this claim that plants grow better by being loved. Buy three identical plants. Label one "the beloved," one "the hated," one "the ignored." Put all three in the same place and give them the same measured amount of food and water each day. For five minutes each day, take "the beloved" down, put it on a table ten feet in front of you and love it. Do nothing physical: don't touch it, breathe on it, or play music to it. Then put it back and put "the hated" plant on the table and hate it for five minutes. Do nothing to "the ignored." After a few months, there should be a measurable difference in growth, if the claim is true.

Even poisonous food can nourish (in small doses) but nothing never nourishes. This is why children from oppressive, tyrannical, or combative families sometimes grow into strong individuals. They have to fight for their identity, and they often win. But children from "I don't care" families seldom learn to care themselves. They may have been cared *for,* but not cared *about;* so they care deeply about nothing. They neither love nor hate; for even hate is a form of caring. Hate is a disease, but indifference is a death.

We can be dead to others, and we can be dead to God, like Job's three friends. Job cares; he both loves and hates God. He calls God his enemy, yet God matters to him even more than his physical pains. But his three "friends" treat God as a safe, respectable object of traditional platitudes. They do not realize, as Job does, that God "is not an uncle. God is an earthquake."[1] Job fights with God; they take flight from God. Job speaks with bitterness and blasphemy, but he speaks *to* God; they speak only *about* God, as if He were absent. They do not realize, as Job does, that "God cannot be expressed, only addressed;"[2] that "God is the only Thou that cannot become an It."[3] That is why God says to them when He finally appears: "I burn with anger against you for not speaking truthfully about Me as My servant Job has done."[4] Fight is more right than flight; a scowl is closer to a smile than a snore. It is at least a face.

Indifference is a dead relationship. We can be dead to others, or to God, or to death. Let us now descend into the terrible, faceless depths of death as a stranger, a dead relationship with death. It is the depth most devoid of light, the faceless face. Yet even here we must bring light; we must face the faceless face. And this exploration of the darkness may unearth some surprising light.

WHY NOT TO "BURY THE DEAD"

There is every reason for not ignoring death. Death is the profoundest fact of life, the most important event in life. No one's death is ordinary. It raises the least of us to greatness, like becoming president—the office enlarges the person. We may not respond heroically, but death is a heroic challenge.

Death is the Great Sphinx. It is intrinsically fascinating, as anything great and unknown is fascinating. The mysterious is fascinating because it invites exploration. It is an "undiscovered country." How fascinated I was as a child by my father's old maps with large white areas marked "unexplored"! We have mapped our planet, but not our life or our death. That is why I am a philosopher.

The unknown fascinates because it is heavy with promises of secrets and surprises. So we question the unusual, not the usual. We do not question why a man enters the bus, but we do question why a giraffe enters the bus. Death is like that giraffe! As we saw in Chapter 1, death is not natural. All our myths wonder at its presence in the human bus. The bus is not its home; death is a stranger who somehow has crept into our home. Heidegger describes it as "a strange and alien *(unheimlich)* thing that banishes us once and for all from everything in which we are at home."[5] He says that our "being-towards-death is essentially anxiety" and that "in anxiety one feels *uncanny (unheimlich)*."[6] The translators note that "uncanny" means more literally 'unhomelike.' "[7] But it means more than "unhomelike" *(ungemütlich);* it means uncanny, even occult. Death is fascinating because it is occult.

Death is more fascinating than a giraffe on a bus because giraffes are occult only in some places, like busses, while death is occult everywhere. Death takes us to the absolute edge of the world. It is like our fascination with the golden fleece at the dark edge of the world, or with "The Well at the World's End."[8] A flat earth is more fascinating than a round earth because a flat earth has an edge, an end, and thus an unknown, occult "un-home" beyond the end. In Tolkien's great myth, *The Silmarillion,* the world is made round as a divine punishment:

> And there is not now upon Earth any place abiding where the memory of a time without evil is preserved. For . . . the world was diminished, for Valinor and Eressëa (the dwellings of the gods) were taken from it into the realm of hidden things . . . and they longed ever to escape from the shadows of their exile and to see in some fashion the light that dies not; for the sorrow of the thought of death had pursued them over the deeps of the sea. Thus it was that great mariners among them would still search the empty seas. . . . But they found it not. And those that sailed far came only to new lands, and found them like to the old lands, and subject to death. And those that sailed furthest set but a girdle about the Earth and returned weary at last to the place of their beginning; and they said: 'All roads are now bent.'[9]

The spatial image is a temporal one too. Round, or cyclic, time would be like a round earth, or curved space: relatively dull and meaningless. Linear time is like a flat earth or a straight road. A flat earth has an edge; a straight road has an end. Our world has no edge in space, but it has an edge in time. Death is the edge, the end. It creates the fascination.

PREMODERN MAN'S FASCINATION WITH DEATH

In *The Courage to Be,* Paul Tillich distinguishes the ancient, medieval, and modern minds by their different fundamental anxieties. Anxiety about meaninglessness is typically modern, says Tillich, anxiety about guilt is typically medieval, and anxiety about death is typically ancient.[10] Another such classification is that the ancient pre-Christian mind was death-accepting (and fatalistic); the medieval Christian mind was death-defying (believing in the resurrection); and the modern post-Christian mind is death-denying (looking away from death as a stranger). In any case, pre-modern man was not death-denying. Throughout the premodern world, man's concern with death was his oldest and most central concern. "The oldest, most numerous and most imposing relics of our ancestors are funerary," says Toynbee.[11]

The Egyptian Book of the Dead is probably mankind's first book. It dates back to the birth of Egyptian civilization, somewhere between 5892 and 4455 B.C. It was written to prepare a person for death and life after death. This is man's oldest philosophy of life, life as the rehearsal for death. It is the view both of the greatest myths and the greatest philosophers.

Medieval man also thought about death. *Memento mori* (remember death) and *respice finem* (look to the end) were medieval maxims. Whatever else death was, it was no stranger then. For centuries people prayed "to be spared a sudden and unprovided death."[12] They feared not thinking about death more than death itself. Today, people *hope* for "a sudden and unprovided death" so that they might *not* have time to think about it. They fear thinking about death more than death itself!

THE MODERN CHRISTIAN IGNORING OF DEATH

Even many Christian preachers and churches treat death as a stranger today. Nothing could be more ironic. When the Christian church collaborates with a pagan culture by covering up death, it seals its own death warrant. For the whole reason for the church's existence, its whole message, is a "good news" or gospel about a God who became man in order to solve the problem of death and the problem of sin, which is its root. Whether the story is true or false, it is fundamentally a story about resurrection from death, conquest of death. The resurrection is the heart of every sermon preached by every Christian in the New Testament. For the church to cover up death is for it to cover up the question whose answer is its own meaning. Nothing is more meaningless than an answer without a question. The "good news" of Christianity claims to answer the "bad news" of death. Without the "bad news," the "good news" sounds like a charming but superfluous fairy tale, a mélange of commonplace ethical platitudes inexplicably encumbered with miracles and mythology, an echo of parental imperatives already long known and disobeyed. The "good news" becomes neither good news nor even news. The Sermon on the Mount does not answer the problem of death. The resurrection does. But the answer presupposes the problem, presupposes facing death as an enemy. No wonder teaching that answer without facing the problem strikes the hearer as irrelevant mythology to be ignored as death is ignored. If the question is a stranger, the answer will be a stranger too.

There is much concern about a "loss of faith" among young people. Death is the test of faith. Any faith that can die, should die, because it not faith but platitude, soporific, or wishful thinking. Real faith cannot be shaken "because it is the result of having been shaken."[13] It is an answer to being shaken. Real answers are answers to real questions. Death is a real question. If faith is a real answer, it must face that real question; it must stand face to face with death. When faith and death thus meet, it is death, not faith, that is changed. "Death, Thou shalt die."[14] But when death and platitudes meet, it is the platitudes that are changed. That is why platitudes fear to face death: they fear their own death in that encounter. And that is why a Christianity minus the resurrection treats death as a stranger.

THE MODERN POST-CHRISTIAN IGNORING OF DEATH

Modern culture is not Christian but post-Christian. Why does it treat death as a stranger? Since previous cultures, pagan as well as

Christian, did not treat death as a stranger, our reasons for doing so must lie in our culture rather than in death itself. What is distinctive about modern culture?

Many things, but at least six of them are reasons for turning death into a stranger. We are (1) collectivistic, (2) skeptical, (3) relativistic, (4) technologistic, (5) hedonistic, and (6) externalistic. Let us see how each works to turn death into a stranger.

Collectivism

We are a collectivist, conformist, stereotyped, "other-directed"[15] culture.* We sometimes think of ourselves as individualists; but it is a lie. It is true that we do not look up to leaders, heroes, or authority figures; but we do not thereby become leaders or heroes ourselves. Sheep without shepherds are still sheep. The great modern experiment of making all the sheep into shepherds by denying the authority of the shepherds has backfired. Instead of replacing the "tradition-directed" person of ancient societies with the "inner-directed" person, the goal of Renaissance individualism, the modern world has replaced him with the "other-directed" person, the faceless crowd. We fear to be alone, perhaps because then we would have to face our facelessness.

But in death we are alone. Only in death are we completely alone. Death is the only completely individual event in our lives. We live together; we die alone. Collectivized man, therefore, cannot face death, for his face is not an individual face, but the face of death is.

But are we not all one in death? Is not death "the great leveller," the great collectivizer? No. We are not "all one in death"; we are *each* one in death. Death individuates. It is true that one skeleton looks pretty much like any other; but a skeleton is not death. It is what becomes of a body after death. What dies is not a skeleton like any other, but an individual unlike any other. Beneath differences that are only skin-deep, skeletons are the same; but there is a level beneath skeletons, the level of character; and contrary to America's most deeply believed dogma, it is simply not true that "deep down we're all the same." That is exactly where we are *not* all the same. We are all different. We are more our unique selves in spirit than in body. Democracy before the law. equa-

---

* At the same time we are lonely individuals, lacking the kind of organic community typified by ancient Athens or medieval Christendom. True individuality and true community stand or fall together.

lity of rights—this is humanizing. But sameness of spirit, Xeroxed souls—this is dehumanizing. If we are copies, we cannot face death, for death is always original. At death we put our signature on our life's unique self-portrait.

Skepticism

We are dogmatic skeptics. Our official dogma is the dogma that there are no dogmas. We are certain only that there is nothing certain. Therefore we avoid thinking about death because we have no answers to the ultimate and uncomfortable question it asks. Many books tell us how to grow up, go to school, attain puberty, get married, have a baby, have a nervous breakdown, get a divorce, get an abortion, change jobs, travel, retire, or fight with our in-laws; but few if any tell us how to die. We approach the most important event of all unprepared. Why? The embarrassingly obvious reason is that we simply do not know what all previous cultures claimed to know, that is, the meaning of death (and, correlatively, the meaning of life).

This also explains our fear of silence. We need noise to distract us from the knowledge of our ignorance of life and death. Life is ultimately meaningless to us; but if there is enough noise we never need hear this terrible silence.

> Faces along the bar
> Cling to their average day:
> The lights must never go out,
> The music must always play . . .
> Lest we should see where we are,
> Lost in a haunted wood,
> Children afraid of the night
> Who have never been happy or good.[16]

Relativism

A corollary of skepticism is relativism. Skepticism means there is no certain *knowledge;* relativism means there is no certain *reality,* no real absolutes. But we are not consistent relativists; we do not ask whether it is only relatively true that everything is relative; we are not relativistic about our relativism. If we were, we would leave room for a possible absolute somewhere. But just as we are dogmatic about our skepticism, we are absolute about our relativism.

Our world view is relativistic not only in terms of space and time (because of Einstein) but also in terms of truth and value (and this is not because of Einstein, though there is a strange confusion in many minds which assumes that if space and time are relative, it logically follows that truth and value are relative too). Our literature lacks an overarching context of meaning. Our stories do not move within a world of objective truths and values. Therefore they have no heroes, for there are no absolutes to be heroic about. The protagonists have no adventures, only incidents, as Roquentin explains in Sartre's *Nausea:* "I have never had adventures. Things have happened to me, events, incidents, anything you like. But no adventures. It isn't a question of words."[17]

Indeed it isn't. If there are no absolutes, there can be no heroism, for there is nothing to be heroic about. Attempted heroism in a world without real absolutes becomes fantasy, foolishness, or fanaticism—Don Quixote or something worse. And if there is no heroism, there can be no adventures. A book like *The Lord of the Rings* is immensely popular in our age not only because it is a masterpiece in any age but also because it offers food to starving souls. It restores adventures by restoring heroism by restoring a world of absolutes. It is an oasis in our desert. For the typically modern novel, life is "full of sound and fury, signifying nothing":

> Tomorrow and tomorrow and tomorrow
> Creeps in this petty pace from day to day
> To the last syllable of recorded time
> And all our yesterdays have lighted fools
> The way to dusty death. Out, out, brief candle!
> Life's but a walking shadow, a poor player
> That struts and frets his hour upon the stage
> And then is heard no more. It is a tale
> Told by an idiot, full of sound and fury,
> Signifying nothing.[18]

What a terrible word, that "nothing." No modern nihilist has put it more starkly or strongly. Paradoxically, it is Shakespeare, embedded in the medieval-Elizabethan universe packed with meaning, who paints a more powerful portrait of meaninglessness than any modern author who inhabits a meaningless world. The reason is the *frame:* Shakespeare's meaningful world framed his portrait of meaninglessness. The above quotation is put into the mouth of a man who is going mad. It is a philosophy framed and judged insane by a sane universe; a life framed and judged meaningless by a meaningful universe. But *Modernity removes the frame,* and presents us with the kind of world in which these insane ravings are true.

All relative meanings are meaningful because they are relative to an absolute meaning. That is the meaning of the word "relative": relative to the nonrelative. Take away any absolute meaning and all relative meanings eventually go too. Modern literature, reflecting modern life, is typically a confession of meaninglessness because it denies any absolute. Or rather, it denies all but one. Even though there are no objective absolutes, even though "God is dead," there is still one subjective absolute: death. When God is dead, death is God.

Our relativism is, at the same time, the reason why we ignore this last absolute and the reason why we are subversively fascinated with it. Our world tells us only of relativities, but our heart still speaks a word that is absolute. The word is death.

It is the last word.

Technologism

Another reason for our estrangement from death is that for two or three centuries our civilization has worshipped at the shrine of technology, of "man's conquest of nature." The difference this new ideal has made cannot be exaggerated; it sets our culture apart from all others at its heart. For all previous cultures, the cardinal problem of human life was to confrom the human self somehow to objective reality (a reality believed to be greater than Man, and to include God, truths, or values); and to do so through such things as wisdom, virtue, or religion. For our culture, the cardinal problem of human life is to conform objective reality to the wishes of Man (for objective reality is now seen as something less than Man, as mere matter; matter is seen as objective, but not values); and we do so through technology. The humanization of nature rather than the divinization of Man is our new *summum bonum.*

This relates to our ignoring of death through the connecting link of a demand for comfort, security, and control. Nietzsche says: "He who has a *why* to live can bear with almost any *how.*"[19] He means that a man can endure upsetting, inconvenient, or painful physical circumstances if only he has a strongly believed purpose, a goal and a meaning to his life. Even a small amount of meaninglessness and purpose-lessness makes suffering unendurable; even a little meaning makes it endurable. Viktor Frankl verified this in the Nazi concentration camps.[20] The prisoners who survived, physically as well as mentally, were the ones who found some meaning in their apparently meaning-less sufferings. Those who did not find a meaning did not survive, even if they were strong in all other ways. The corollary of "He who has a *why* to live can bear with almost any *how*" is surely that "He who does *not* have a *why* to live can*not* bear with almost any *how*." Modern man fits that corollary. If he believes in no purpose to his life higher than worldly success and pleasure (the end to which technological control over material nature is a means), then he cannot endure suffering. He is soft. He demands a degree of comfort and security unheard of in pre-modern cultures because without it his sufferings, no longer meaning-ful, would be unendurable. It is not simply that since he now has the comfort dispensers of technology, he naturally takes advantage of them. They came to him not as a gift from heaven or chance but from his own demand for power, for control over nature. This need was the source of technology; technology was not the source of the need. And these new needs for *hows* arose from the loss of his *whys*.

What does this have to do with death? Toynbee puts it this way:

> If the fact of death were once admitted to be a reality even in the United States, then it would have to be admitted that the United States is not the earthly paradise that it is deemed to be (and this is one of the crucial articles of faith in "the American way of life").[21]

In *Civilization and Its Discontents* Freud comments that through technology modern man has fulfilled most of the dreams of premodern man, the dreams he wishfully projected into his gods. He can now do nearly everything a god can do. Then he asks a simple but profound question: *Why is he not happy?*[22] At least part of the answer must be that a god is immortal. The fact of death is the failure of our dream of divinity. No wonder we turn our face from it. Death's face grins at us, and we must frown. In order to put a smile on our face, we must put the mask of a stranger on the face of death.

Hedonism

The fact that we must put a smile on our face, the fact that we de-mand happiness, is another reason our culture ignores death. We are

hedonists. We seek happiness not in the ancient sense of objective perfection (*eudaimonia*) but in the modern sense of subjective contentment,
being pleased. This is a happiness indistinguishable from pleasure except by degree of depth and endurance. We worship "life, liberty, and
the pursuit of happiness," not life after death, the service of God, and
the pursuit of truth. We prefer happiness to truth. That is why we do
not think about death.

We humans have innate drives for both truth and happiness, for
both adventure and contentment, both exploration and at-home-ness.
In those whom William James calls the "tough-minded," the first
drive predominates; in the "tender-minded," the second.[23] We are a
predominantly "tender-minded" culture. The thought of death exerts
opposite influences on these two minds: on the tough mind, the
fascination of unknown truth; on the tender mind, the fear of unknown
unhappiness. Since each of us has both a tough mind and a tender
mind, death exerts contrary influences on us. If one of our two minds is
suppressed, however, death's corresponding influence is suppressed.
Therefore, a tender-minded individual or culture fears and avoids
death even while its suppressed tough mind is fascinated with it.

Modern man is coming more and more to this point. It is the point of
Nietzsche's prophetic portrait of "the last man":

> Thus spoke Zarathustra to the people: "The time has come for man to set
> himself a goal. The time has come for man to plant the seed of his highest
> hope. His soil is still rich enough. But one day this soil will be poor and
> domesticated, and no tall tree will be able to grow in it. Alas, the time is
> coming when man will no longer shoot the arrow of his longing beyond
> man, and the string of his bow will have forgotten how to whir! . . .
>
> "Alas, the time is coming when man will no longer give birth to a star.
> Alas, the time of the most despicable man is coming, he that is no longer
> able to despise himself. Behold, I show you the *last man*.
>
> "'What is love? What is creation? What is longing? What is a star?' thus
> asks the last man, and he blinks.
>
> "The earth has become small, and on it hops the last man, who makes
> everything small. His race is as ineradicable as the flea-beetle; the last man
> lives longest.
>
> "'We have invented happiness,' say the last men, and they blink. . . .
>
> "One still works, for work is a form of entertainment. But one is careful
> lest the entertainment be too harrowing. One no longer becomes poor or
> rich: both require too much exertion. Who still wants to rule? Who obey?
> Both require too much exertion.

"No shepherd and one herd! Everybody wants the same, everybody is the same: whoever feels different goes voluntarily into a madhouse.

"'Formerly, all the world was mad,' say the most refined, and they blink.

"One is clever and knows everything that has ever happened; so there is no end of derision. One still quarrels, but one is soon reconciled—else it might spoil the digestion.

'One has one's little pleasure for the day and one's little pleasure for the night: but one has a regard for health.

"'We have invented happiness,' say the last men, and they blink."

And here ended Zarathustra's first speech, which is also called "The Prologue"; for at this point he was interrupted by the clamor and delight of the crowd. "Give us this last man, O Zarathustra," they shouted. "Turn us into these last men!"[24]

The "last man . . . lives longest" because he knows not death. In his mind, he lives forever and never dies, and therefore never really lives. He has slipped past the seraphim's flaming sword back into Eden; the sword is death. But it is the backward step. Eden is no longer paradise for humans, that is, for mortals. "You can't go home again." God does not let Himself be found there any more. Once man vacates Eden, God does too. Life is now to be found only "East of Eden," through conflict and challenge and suffering, through history and time and death.

Death is the supreme conflict, the conflict with ourselves, the event in which the self is put into question and apparently fails the test, loses, dies. Conflict is not pleasant. Therefore our pleasure-loving culture avoids conflict, especially the supreme conflict.

Externalism

The deepest reason of all for our estrangement from death is our externalism. We are not a meditative, contemplative, thoughtful people. We live outside ourselves, not inside ourselves; we think the cultivation of the "inner life" fit only for monks and mystics. We identify ourselves by our relationships, our social roles, our activities. The first thing we ask about someone is "What does he *do?*" Though we like to "express our feelings," they are seldom our deep feelings; we express our feelings but not our *selves*. We know our breadth but not our depth.

In fact, we fear our inner selves. If we are put into a dark, silent room for one hour, free from all diversions and forced to meet ourselves, we are either bored or terrified. We are so bored that even if the dullest person we ever met were there in that room with us for that hour, we would not be so completely bored. Does this mean we find ourselves more boring than the most boring person we ever met? That the most boring person we ever met is ourselves? Or else we are terrified, because when the dark room forces us to take off our masks and roles and relationships and enter into ourselves, we may discover that there is No One There! It is like a very bad "knock, knock" joke:

"Knock, knock."
"Who's there?"
"Nobody."
"Nobody who?"
"Nobody *you.*"

Being alone with ourselves is threatening to us because we are not sure we *are* selves. We are terrified of the nightmare of meeting The Man With No Face in the mirror. That is why we invent so many diversions.

We seek diversion because we fear being alone with ourselves. But in death, as in the dark room, we are alone with ourselves. Death is a dark room bigger than the universe and smaller than an atom. We fear it and turn it into a stranger because if we are not sure we are selves in life, we cannot be sure we are selves in death. Death forces us into the dark room, as life does not. When we are in the light rooms of life, we need not look at ourselves because there is so much else to look at. In the dark room there is only ourselves. Looking at death is like looking *at* nothing, but looking *into* a mirror. In ordinary knowing, we can forget the knower. Gabriel Marcel calls ordinary knowing "problems" and the knowing that is like looking into a mirror "mysteries."[25] A "mystery" is a question whose object is the subject, the asker; a question in which I am involved, not detached. Love, evil, the union of body and soul, and death are examples of mysteries. Mathematics, tree surgery, and butterfly collecting are examples of problems.

An individual or a culture can choose to look into the mirror of mystery, or it can choose to look away. The ancient Greeks were a great culture because they chose to look. The command written over the Delphic oracle was "Know thyself"; and heroes like Oedipus and Socrates paid a high price for this knowledge: the sacrifice of security, satisfaction, and even (in Socrates' case) life itself. Our culture will not pay the price. John Stuart Mill said, "It is better to be a human being dissatisfied than a pig satisfied, better to be Socrates dissatisfied than a fool satisfied."[26] We are the pig people.

But death forces us out of our pigskins. At death we can no longer look away from ourselves into a boob tube; we must look into the mirror. We must see and say who we are. Before death there are three possible answers to every question: yes, no, and evasion. Death removes the third answer.

Before death, evasion is always possible, that is, evasion of self, and therefore evasion of death, since death forces us to face ourselves. But evasion of death takes effort. A stark and massive thing like death is like a mountain, not easily hidden. Even when it is sanitized, anaesthetized, homogenized, mechanized, and institutionalized in hospitals— even when it is taken from our sight, it is not taken from our ken because it is our kin. How is evasion possible? How can we face death as a stranger if we know it?

Here the externalized mind plays its trump card. There are two meanings to "know." We may know *that* something is true, or we may *know* that something. We may know *about* someone, or we may *know* that someone. We may have *savoir* or *connaître, wissen* or *kennen,* knowledge by description or knowledge by acquaintance, secondhand knowledge or firsthand knowledge. The externalized mind's trump card is to substitute knowledge about death for knowing death.

This substitution works in two ways. First, to escape the personal and individual knowledge that "I will die," we substitute the impersonal and general knowledge that "all men are mortal," that "people die." (But I am not "people"; I am *this person.*) Second, we admit the death of another ("He will die") but not of ourselves. (But I am not "he"; I am *I.*) I thus keep my distance from death.

The second way has a subtle twist to it. I can even look at myself as an object, as a "he," and thus admit death into that self while yet keeping my distance from it. For I am both "I" and "he," both subject and object, both look*er* and looked-*at.* I admit death into my "he" but not into my "I." I can thus admit death's presence into myself and still evade the personal truth of death if the only side of myself I look at is the objective side; I look at myself as an ingredient in the world, one of many human beings, with this name, this family, these thoughts, and so forth. But who is it that *has* this name, this family, these thoughts?

Who goes there? The name will die; the objective entity will die; the thing seen and known as an object will die; but the see-er and knower, the *I,* is not this object but this subject. Must *I* face death? By forgetting myself as subject, I neatly avoid the face-to-face encounter with death: I let my mask face it instead.

The classic text in modern literature on the denial of death is Tolstoy's short story "The Death of Ivan Ilyitch." Watch Ivan play on himself all the tricks we have just mentioned.

> Ivan Ilyitch saw that he was going to die, and he was in perpetual despair.
>
> In the depths of his soul, Ivan Ilyitch knew that he was going to die; but he not only failed to get used to the thought, but also simply did not comprehend it, could not comprehend it.
>
> This form of syllogism which he had studied in Kiziveter's "Logic"— "Kai is a man, men are mortal, therefore Kai is mortal,"—had seemed to him all his life true only in its application to Kai, but never to himself. It was Kai as man, as man in general, and in this respect it was perfectly correct; but he was not Kai, and not man in general, and he had always been an entity absolutely, absolutely distinct from all others: he had been Vanya with mamma and papa, with Mitya and Volodya, with his playthings, the coachman, with the nurse; then with Katenka, with all the joys, sorrows, enthusiasms of childhood, boyhood, youth.
>
> Was it Kai who smelt the odor of the little striped leather ball that Vanya loved so dearly? Was it Kai who kissed his mother's hand? and was it for Kai that the silken folds of his mother's dress rustled so? Was it he who made a conspiracy for the tarts at the Law School.? Was it Kai who had been so in love? Was it Kai who had such ability in conducting the sessions?
>
> "And Kai is certainly mortal, and it is proper that he should die; but for me, Vanya, Ivan Ilyitch, with all my feelings, my thoughts—for me, that is another thing, and it cannot be that I must take my turn and die. That would be too horrible."
>
> This was the way that he felt about it:
>
> "If I were going to die, like Kai, then, surely, I should have known it; some internal voice would have told me; but nothing of the sort happened in me, and I myself, and my friends, all of us, perceived that it was absolutely different in our case from what it was with Kai. But now how is it?" he said to himself. "It cannot be, it cannot be, but it is! How is this? How understand it?"
>
> And he could not understand it; and he endeavored to put away this thought as false, unjust, unwholesome, and to supplant it with other

thoughts true and wholesome. But this thought, not merely as a thought, but, as it were, a reality, kept recurring and taking form before him.

And he summoned in place of this thought other thoughts, one after the other, in the hope of finding succor in them. He strove to return to his former course of reasoning, which hid from him of old the thought of death. But strangely enough, all that which formerly hid, concealed, destroyed the image of death, was now incapable of producing that effect. . . . Ivan Ilyitch perceived it, tried to turn his thoughts from it; but it took its course, and it came up and stood directly before him, and gazed at him: and he was stupefied; the fire died out in his eyes, and he began once more to ask himself,

"Is there nothing true save IT?"[27]

The stranger Ivan has run from all his life is his other self, his *Doppelgänger*, his death-self; and when it catches up with him, it is as a stranger, as IT.

I can experience the death of another as an object, but not my death; my death is not an object because I am not an object. But if I admit only what I can experience, then I will not admit my own death. (Nor will I admit my own *I*-self! Death-realization is the index of self-realization.) Admitting the death of others cannot bring me one step closer to admitting my own; it may even bring me many steps away. Undertakers, embalmers, or writers of obituaries (or books about death!) can ignore death more effectively than other people, for their very livelihood involves objectifying it.

THE PORNOGRAPHY OF DEATH

Entertainment media that trade in violence also make their living by objectifying death. They treat death in the same way that pornography treats sex: as an IT. Sexual pornography means seeing the human body merely as an object of sexual desire and gratification, not as an instrument of the self, the subject, the soul. Such "soul-categories" as promise, choice, commitment, and even love are suppressed or trivialized. But this is the deepest meaning of sexuality—it is something we *are* in our souls, our inner beings, not just something we *do* with our bodies.

In the same way, death is portrayed pornographically in movies, TV, popular fiction, even the news. It is depersonalized, made the object of curiosity or sensationalism. It is externalized. It is a way of forgetting or fleeing death, as sexual pornography is a way of fleeing true sexuality; this is why both pornographies are popular with people who have fears and hangups about death or sex.

The denial of death is one reason for our tolerance of violence. We watch violence on a TV screen or in movies detachedly, from a distance, as the Romans watched the gladitorial contests. *What we watch is not ourselves.* Turning it into an object exorcizes it from our inner being. We are not involved, not responsible; we are spectators, not participants. Death becomes tolerable when it happens to others.

But when we have made death a spectator sport, we have made life a spectator sport. To be detached from our death is to be detached from our life.

One form of detachment is our amoralism. We are not an immoral but an amoral culture. And our denial of death is connected with this. We would have to be involved in life and in death to be moral; for to be moral is to make moral judgments, and we do not like to make moral judgments. A judgment is an act, an involvement, a commitment, a stand. The self has to come out of hiding to make a judgment. Berdyayev puts the connection between moral judgments and death this way:

> A system of ethics which does not make death its central problem . . . is lacking in depth and earnestness. Although it deals with judgments and valuations, it forgets about the final judgment and valuation, i.e. about the Last Judgment.[28]

"JAWS" AS DEATH

No matter how much we consciously flee from the face of death, we subconsciously know it. The spectacular box office success of the movie *Jaws* stems from this fact. *Jaws* is an image of death, of true death, of our own death. That is why it is so fascinating, especially to a society that hides this aspect of death. The open, empty jaws of the inhuman beast from the mysterious ocean depths speak a message of death quite different from that spoken by a soldier's bullet, or a speeding car, or a disease. It is uncanny; it is dark; it is nothing. The jaws are jaws of *nothingness.*

Death is a nothingness, not a somethingness. The death of another is a something, an object, an event in my world and in my life. I observe it as an object and live through it. But my own death is not a something, a finite object or event *in* a world and a life. It is the end of a world and a life. When I look into my own death, I look into emptiness, as into Jaws.

The distinction between death as objective and death as subjective is also the distinction between death as natural and death as unnatural, which we discovered in Chapter 1. *Jaws* presents death as the old myths do, as unnatural, as uncanny, as a shock—or a shark. The scientific attitude is the objective attitude; therefore, it is the scientist who sees death as natural—and the scientist in *Jaws* who sees the shark as just another natural species to be killed. It is the captain who knows with deeper instincts, as Ahab knew Moby Dick. The captain's knowledge of death (Jaws) is a foreknowledge; He knows that it is stronger. He knows death by dying. It is the only way. At the moment of death, at least, no one is a scientist.

A DILEMMA AND A DEAD END

We have looked at two ways of looking at death. The first sees Death as (1) subjective, (2) private, (3) individual, (4) unnatural, (5) nothingness, and (6) an enemy. The second sees it as (1) objective, (2) public, (3) universal, (4) natural, (5) something, and (6) a stranger.

We seem to be impaled on the horns of a dilema. Do we see death as an enemy or as a stranger? The first seems to end in despair; the second, in dishonesty. We seem to have come to a dead end.

AN ESCAPE FROM ESCAPISM

Seeing death as a starnger is escapism. We want to escape from escapism, but not back to despair. The only other direction is forward. Let us look further *into* escapism instead of backing away; perhaps we will find there, as we found in Chapter 1, a light in the deepest part of the darkness. Perhaps there is a deeper meaning and a clue in our coverup of death, a deeper meaning than mere escapism and a clue to the meaning of death itself. Let's look.

We "bury our dead" away in hospitals, but every culture buries its dead in the earth. The substitution of the hospital for the earth is significant, surely, but so is the common burial. Why have we always buried our dead? Even animals seek seclusion when death approaches. Are they practicing dishonesty and escapism? Or do they perhaps have some unconscious anticipation of the same instinctive wisdom we have, the instinct to turn away from the public world to the private world at death because that is the world in which death reveals its true meaning? We instinctively cover our faces or turn away from death— why? Perhaps because we know with our hearts that death is a great mystery not open to public and outward observation; that the truth of death is not what the eyes can see, that apperances are deceving. Might it be that we bury the deceitful appearances of death not to be deceived but to be undeceived? That we bury the dead not to escape the true meaning of death but to find it by escaping the false, external meaning of death? We cover our faces—is it to transform our hands into a mirror, to turn from the death of the other to our own death? For here, only to the closed eye is there true vision; the open eye is empty and fatuous. The fathoms open inward.

If this is why we bury our dead, we are wise. We do not see death. A dead body is not death. We see the dead body of another; we can never see our own dead body. For the eyes are dead when the body is dead. Therefore we turn from the body of death in order to see death truly.

No individual and no culture can look directly into the face of death and see anything. Looking at death is like looking at nothing—*or like looking at the sun.* Which is it? Perhaps we see nothing when we look at death truly (our own death), not because death is so dark but because death is so bright! It may be that looking at death is like looking at the sun. We can look at it face to face only for a split second and then we must turn away or go blind. Like Oedipus we have no eyes to bear that sight. Like Empedocles on Etna we look into the volcano and die. Death, like God, says, "No man can see my face and live."

If this is the reason we cannot look death in the face, then it is the very excess of light that blinds us. Death seems dark to us not because it is dark (empty, nothing, meaningless) but because it is so full of light (being, fullness, meaning).

We have seen that death (true death) is not an object. Light is also not an object. Light is not lit. Perhaps death is not lit because it is like light. Perhaps we could not find the truth of death because death is the source of truth. We were trying to light up the sun with a sunbeam.

But if death is light, if death is the source of truth, then death is neither enemy nor stranger but friend. For light and truth are our friends. As water is the throat's friend and food the stomach's friend, so light is the friend of the eye, and truth of the mind.

Let us follow this clue. It is only a clue, a possibility. It is not proved—few things are. But it is a chink of light, a door slightly ajar, a sign along the road. If we do not follow it we are lost. Even if we *do* follow it, we may be lost. There is no guarantee. But we have no other place to go.

NOTES

1. Abraham Heschel, quoted in Joseph Needleman, *The New Religions* (New York: Pocket Books, 1970), p. 6: "I recall one winter afternoon years ago in New York discussing Jewish mystical communities with the great scholar Abraham Heschel at a time when he was working on the translation of a particular Hasidic text. He pounded his finger on a stack of manuscripts in front of him and quoted something he had just translated: 'God is not nice. He is not an uncle. God is an earthquake.' "

2. Martin Buber, *I And Thou*, trans. Walter Kaufmann (New York: Charles Scribner's Sons, 1970), p. 129. Compare the older Ronald Gregor Smith translation.

3. Ibid., p. 160.

4. Job 42:7 (Jerusalem Bible).

5. Martin Heidegger, *An Introduction to Metaphysics,* trans. by Ralph Manheim (New York: Doubleday, Anchor, 1961), p. 133.

6. Martin Heidegger, *Being and Time* (New York: Harper & Row, 1962), pp. 310, 233.

7. Ibid. The test reads: In der Angst ist einem 'unheimlich.' " The footnote explains: "While 'unheimlich' is here translated as 'uncanny,' it means more literally 'unhomelike,' as the author proceeds to point out." This refers to Heidegger's statement on p. 233 that "here 'uncanniness' also means 'not-being-at-home.' "

8. William Morris, *The Well at the World's End* (New York: Ballantine, 1978).

9. J.R.R. Tolkien, *The Silmarillion* (Boston: Houghton Mifflin, 1977), p. 281.

10. Paul Tillich, *The Courage to Be* (New Haven: Yale University Press, 1966).

11. Arnold Toynbee et. al., *Man's Concern with Death* (New York: McGraw-Hill, 1969), pp. 59-60.

12. From the Litany of the Saints.

13. Abraham Heschel (source unknown).

14. John Donne, "Death Be Not Proud." In *The Complete Poetry of John Donne*, ed. J. T. Shawcross (New York: New York University Press, 1968).

15. Cf. David Riesman, *The Lonely Crowd* (New Haven: Yale University Press, 1950).

16. W. H. Auden, "September 1, 1939." In *Collected Poetry of W. H. Auden* (New York: Random House, 1945; London: Faber & Faber, 1976).

17. Jean-Paul Sartre, *Nausea* (New York: New Directions, 1959), p. 53.

18. Shakespeare, *Macbeth*, act 5, scene 5, lines 19-28.

19. Friedrich Nietzsche quoted in Viktor Frankl, *Man's Search for Meaning* (New York: Washington Square Press, 1963), p. 121.

20. Frankl, *Man's Search.*
21. Toynbee, *Man's Concern,* p. 13.
22. Sigmund Freud, *Civilization and Its Discontents,* trans. James Strachey (New York: W. W. Norton, 1961), pp. 41–47.
23. William James, "Pragmatism," in *Pragmatism and Other Essays* (New York: Washington Square Press, 1963), p. 9.
24. Friedrich Nietzsche, *Thus Spake Zarathsutra,* trans. R. J. Hollingdale (Baltimore: Penguin Books, 1961), First Part, sec. 5.
25. Gabriel Marcel, "On the Ontological Mystery," in *The Philosophy of Existentialism,* trans. Manya Harari (New York: Citadel Press, 1956), p. 19.
26. John Stuart Mill, "Utilitarianism," in *Essays on Ethics, Religion and Society by John Stuart Mill,* ed. J. M. Robson (Toronto: University of Toronto Press, 1969), p. 212.
27. Leo Tolstoy, *The Death of Ivan Ilyitch and Other Stories,* trans. Aylmer Mande (New York: New American Library, 1960), pp. 131–133.
28. N. Berdyayev, *The Destiny of Man* (New York: Harper & Row, 1960), p. 263.

CHAPTER 3

Death as a Friend

A friend is more than a stranger or an enemy, but less than a mother or a lover. Seeing death as a friend is the middle step of our journey into death. It is a forward step, but it is not the final step as it is in most current books on death. Such books usually sidestep the issue of life after death. When we look at death as a mother and as a lover, we will confront that issue; but not yet. We cannot explore these two faces, which lie beyond or behind the face of death as a friend, until we explore the face of death as a friend itself. Naturalistic philosophies of death may sidestep death's supernatural faces, but a supernaturalistic philosophy of death will not sidestep any of death's natural faces.

Death is our friend for seven reasons: It is our being, our openness, our life's frame, our appreciation of life, our food, our truth, and our opportunity for heroism.

OUR "BEING-TOWARD-DEATH"

If we treat death as a stranger, we treat ourselves as strangers, for death is ourselves. Our very being is a "being-towards-death."[1] This is a fact about our present being, not just about our future. Death is not like the last point on a line, but like the movement and direction of the whole line. We are dying *now*. "In the midst of life, we are in death."[2]

But this is astonishing (if only we let ourselves be astonished by the familiar). It is a paradox, for death means *non*being, nonliving; and now we see nonbeing at the heart of our being, death at the heart of our life. We saw in Chapter 1 that death was an enemy, an other. Now this other turns up at the heart of our self. Death is the black hole in our personal universe; or, conversely, the black holes discovered by astronomers are images of death. Like death, they suck all the being and life in the universe down into themselves, never to return. And they are the enemy within. We have black holes within our very being, our "being-toward-death."

This is terrible. Death is the monster we are, not just the monster we fear; it is not just the enemy but the enemy within. But this realization is also a possible step towards hope. Twice before, at the end of each chapter, we saw hope emerge from the depths, *de profundis;* and here we see it happening again. For the presence of death in the self seems to be a clue that death may be a friend, since a friend too is an other at the heart of the Self. "A friend is another self."[3] A friend is not an It but a Thou, not an object but a subject. I do not merely look *at* a friend *through* my own eyes, as an object in my world; but I look through his eyes at the world and also at myself.[4] A friend is my other self.

But it is a fallacy to argue simply: A friend is an other self; death is an other self; therefore, death is a friend. (Logic students will recognize this as the fallacy of undistributed middle term.) A cancer in a body is also like an other self to that body. It is inside rather than outside. But it is not therefore that body's friend. "Insideness" is a necessary but not sufficient condition for friendship. A second condition is that this other self be a helper, not a harmer; a medicine, not a disease; a friend *and not an enemy.* But death *is* an enemy. How then can it be a friend?

Unless . . . perhaps it is a friend precisely by being an enemy. Like a sparring partner, sometimes we need a friend to act the part of an enemy. Perhaps death is the one we spar with, duel with, test ourselves against, and thereby we grow, prove our mettle, put on spiritual muscle, become our solid selves. Although it is cowardice to "make friends with the *necessity* of dying," it is courage to make friends with death; that is like stepping into the boxing ring.

OPENNESS

Death remains our enemy or our stranger if we refuse that ring, if we see life as a bath, not a battle; a comfortable chair, not a challenge to combat. If we sink back nostalgically into our past, as though it were a warm bath, if we try to arrest the flow of time and change, we cannot see death as a friend; for whatever else death does, "it brings on many changes."[5] It is a cold shower, not a warm bath; it is a slap in the face, a surprise, an interruption.

If we identify ourselves with our future, however; if we love newness, adventure, challenge, creativity, and surprise; then death can become our friend, for it is our greatest adventure. It is always the other, the surprising, that is adventurous—other countries, other peoples, other ideas. And death is the supreme other. The otherness at the heart of our being can be the supreme fascination and our friend if we are open to it.

Openness to otherness—that is not only an attitude toward death but also toward people and toward truth. Love and knowledge are the two supreme forms of openness to otherness. Love and knowledge are therefore our "rehearsal for Death."[6] The priority of these two values is confirmed by two impressive sources: all the great wise men throughout time, and resuscitated patients who seem to have seen the same startlingly similar something when they were medically "dead." It is an impressive piece of prime facie evidence that there exists such a unanimity of testimony within these two groups of people, unorganized as they are and far apart in history, geography, age, temperament, and religion—unanimity in insisting that in the light of death, love and knowledge emerge as life's two supreme values.

It is especially love that prepares us for death because its openness can be reciprocated and reinforced by those we love. How does love prepare us for death? It is not that love constructs merit badges that demand eternal rewards in the name of justice. That's too external. Rather, love constructs a human self that is stronger than death.

How does this work? How does love construct a self that is stronger than death? It constructs my *I*, not my *me;* my subject self, not my object self, *who* I am, not *what* I am. What I am is determined by my heredity and environment; my without is determined from without. This is not stronger than death. But who I am is determined by my free choices to love or not to love; my within is determined from within. This inner self, or who, is not of a given size, like the body, but is elastic. I am as much as I find my identity in, or identify with, or care about, or love. I am not a little ego imprisoned in a bag of skin; I am as big as my love. By my love I construct the self that is stronger than death.

This idea—that love constructs a self that is stronger than death—seems to be taught in the New Testament. For instance, put together the following two passages:

> Love never ends. As for prophecies, they will pass away. As for tongues, they will cease. As for knowledge, it will pass away. For our knowledge is imperfect and our prophecy is imperfect; but when the perfect comes, the imperfect will pass away.
>
> His voice then shook the earth; but now he has promised, "Yet once more I will shake not only the earth but also the heaven." This phrase, "Yet once more," indicates the removal of what is shaken, as of what has been made, in order that what cannot be shaken may remain. Therefore, let us be grateful for receiving a kingdom that cannot be shaken.[7]

The "kingdom that cannot be shaken" is the "love" that "never ends." The fire of death burns away everything that is mortal; the destruction of death destroys everything destructible, shakes everything shakeable. The one indestructible thing is the fire that is greater than the fire of death—the fire of love. Death is a friend because it purifies. It burns away all that is not love. It burns away our closedness and leaves only our openness; it burns away our closets and leaves our front doors—that is, it burns the doors and leaves the doorways. Through death we become open doorways. Insofar as we identify ourselves with open doorways in life, death is our friend.

A FRAME FOR LIFE

A picture needs a frame. A frame is its picture's friend. Death is our life's frame. That is how it is our friend.

Consider the way a frame creates a picture. Suppose the Mona Lisa had no frame, and extended out into the room, and the next room, with other people in it, and the next house, and the next town, and the next country, and the next planet—it would no longer be the Mona Lisa. It would be everything—and therefore nothing. It would be everything in general and therefore nothing in particular.

If there were no death, we would be like that—a picture without a frame; everything, and therefore nothing. Our infinite time would be like the picture's infinite space. One way of removing our frame would be to achieve artificial immortality. Suppose the geneticists come through on their threat (they call it a promise). Many think it can be done by reprogramming human genes not to age, as cancer cells do not age. Suppose you had billions of years and millions of lives. Who would you be? You would wear a million masks, and there would be no one in particular under them. The masks would have an identity because they are finite and mortal; but you would not. You could "be" Napoleon, Josephine, Einstein, Attila the Hun, St. Francis, Woody Allen, Moses, Hugh Hefner, Cleopatra, Marv Thornberry, Socrates, Elvis, and John Doe; but who would you really be? Death alone asks that ultimate question and forces an answer out of us. For "being-there reaches its wholeness in death."[8] "Being-there" (*dasein*) means being-*here,* "being-in-the-world." Even if there is a life after death, still be-ing-*here* reaches its wholeness in death. Without death we could not be whole. Without death there would be no self.

Sheldon Vanauken, in his shattering, moving, and wonderful book *A Severe Mercy,* speaks of this wholeness of self:

> That wholeness can *only* be gained by death, I believe. In writing . . . of my understanding of this astonishing phenomenon, I used the analogy of read-ing a novel like *David Copperfield* that covers many years. In that book one follows the boy David running away to his Aunt Betsy Trotwood, the youth David loving Dora, the mature David with Agnes. While one reads, chapter by chapter, even as one lives one's own life week by week, David is what he is at that particular point in the book's time. But then, when one shuts the book at the end, *all* the Davids—small boy, youth, man—are equally close: and, indeed, are *one.* The *whole* David. One is then, with reference to the book's created time, in an eternity, seeing it all in one's own Now, even as God in His eternal Now sees the whole of history that was and is and will be. But if, as the result of death, I was now seeing the whole Davy at once, I was having a heavenly or eternal vision of her. Only, in heaven I would not have vision only but *her*—whole . . . *all* the Davys began to flow back to me shortly after her death, and I recovered the wholeness of her. . . . It is some-times said that the fourth dimension is time or duration: one does not see a person or thing in any one instant of seeing. . . . As nearly as a lover can do, I was seeing the whole of her.[9]

Another way of seeing this is to suppose you were never born (for birth, like death, frames you and makes you finite). If you were never born, you would have no age. If no one were born, no one would be older or younger than anyone else. You would be no one's parent and no one's child. You would be almost no one.

Death is necessary for life as silence is necessary for speech. It frames it and gives it its wholeness and its significance. Kierkegaard saw this:

> The present state of the world and the whole of life is diseased. If I were a doctor and were asked for my advice I should reply: Create silence! Bring men to silence. The Word of God cannot be heard in the noisy world of to-day. And even if it were blazoned forth with all the panoply of noise so that it could be heard in the midst of all the other noises, then it would no longer be the Word of God. Therefore create silence.[10]

Death creates silence.

The dying often seek out silence. They increasingly withdraw from friends and family, and even from the one most loved. Too often, this withdrawal is misunderstood. It is a time for silence, not speech, for the frame, not the picture. At death you want to ask "What is the meaning of my life, now that it is whole?" You reach the border and see the whole. A student put it this way in a paper:

> On the basis of other life experiences, I find that when a momentous change is about to take place, I closet myself with the thought of it ... The days and particularly the night before my marriage I had a very difficult time talking to anyone ... acquaintance, friend, intimate, or fiance. ... I needed to discover the specific facets within myself that I would draw from my pre-marriage life on through into the marriage ... to distill all the vapors into a condensate of *me*. This I took with me. The same action may be in part what takes place when people withdraw in preparation for death.

APPRECIATION OF LIFE

A fourth reason death is a friend follows from the third. As silence not only allows there to be speech but also allows us to appreciate speech; and as a frame allows us to appreciate the picture it frames; so death allows us to appreciate life. The realization of our mortality *now* jolts us into a new appreciation of the *now*. In Walter de la Mare's words, "Look thy last on all things lovely every hour."[11]

Only from the perspective of death can we fully appreciate life, because appreciation requires perspective, and distance, and comparison. Only from the air can we fully appreciate the land. Only after space travel can we fully appreciate planet Earth. Only a supernaturalist can fully appreciate nature. C. S. Lewis puts it this way:

> The Englishness of English is audible only to those who know some other language as well. In the same way and for the same reason, only Supernaturalists really see Nature. You must go a little away from her, and then turn round, and look back. Then at last the true landscape will become visible. You must have tasted, however briefly, the pure water from beyond the world before you can be distinctly conscious of the hot, salty tang of Nature's current.[12]

This answers a basic objection to thinking about death: that it is "morbid," that it sucks the vitality out of living, that it is unworldly and disloyal to the world to think of its end and ours. The answer to this objection is that exactly the opposite is true. It is not morbid to think of death; it is morbid never to think of death! Life without death is morbid, for it is an empty life, a dead life.

When anything becomes truly a matter of life or death to you, only then do you truly appreciate it; only then do you give it your whole attention and devotion; only then do you give it life. "Death is the salt that gives life its tasty sting," says Kazantzakis.[13]

> The flowers, the fields, and the mountains stood in all their vivid reality before us. . . . A man stood looking at them and thought of his own death and of how he would one day see all this no more. In the moment when he thought of death, he was jolted out of this present reality, and looked at the flowers, the meadow, and the trees as if already from the land of death. They now looked as if he were seeing them through the wrong end of a telescope: far away and very tiny, like toys, and hovering in the distance. They were beautiful as never before.[14]

If we live each day as if it were our last, then when we die we will have no regrets, no "if only I had . . ." We regret not having lived to the fullest because we forget we must die. Viktor Frankl put it this way: "So live as if you were living already for the second time and as if you had just acted the first time as unwisely as you are about to act now."[15] ". . . as if you were living already for the second time"—what does that mean? Abraham Maslow knew.

The editors of *Psychology Today* wrote a brief note after the death of Dr. Abraham Maslow. In it they remarked that he had "a joyful affirmation of life that surged through the long tapes he often dictated for us . . . we did not understand the source of his courage—until the last cassette came in."

On that tape, they say, Dr. Maslow "talked with intense introspection about an earlier heart attack that had come right after he completed an important piece of work. 'I had really spent myself. This was the best I could do, and here was not only a good time to die but I was even willing to die. . . . It was . . .' the completion of the act." It was like a good ending, a good close. I think actors and dramatists have that sense of the right moment for a good ending. . . .

My attitude toward life changed. The word I used for it now is the post-mortem life. I could just as easily have died, so that my living constitutes a kind of extra, a bonus. It's all gravy. Therefore I might just as well live as if I had already died.

One very important aspect of the post-mortem life is that everything gets doubly precious, gets piercingly important. You get stabbed by things, by flowers and by babies and by beautiful things—just the very fact of living, of walking and breathing and eating and having friends and chatting. Everything seems to look more beautiful rather than less, and one gets the much-intensified sense of miracles.

I guess you could say that the post-mortem life permits a kind of spontaneity that's greater than anything else could make possible.

If you're reconciled with death . . . then every single moment of every single day is transformed because the pervasive undercurrent—the fear of death—is removed. . . . I am living an end-life where everything ought to be an end in itself.' "[16]

Notice the connection between the two meanings of "end" in "an end-life": In a life conscious of its temporal end in death, everything is seen as an end in itself, that is, as something intrinsically valuable. Emily realizes this in Thornton Wilder's play *Our Town*. When she sees her past life from the perspective of death (she has just died), she says to the Stage Manager:

I can't. I can't go on. Oh! Oh! It goes so fast. We don't have time to look at one another . . . I didn't realize. So all that was going on and we never noticed. Take me back—up the hill—to my grave. But first: Wait! One more look. Good-by, Good-by, world. Good-by, Grover's Corners . . . Mama and Papa. Good-by to clocks ticking . . . and Mama's sunflowers. And food and coffee. And new ironed dresses and hot baths . . . and sleeping and waking up. Oh, earth, you're too wonderful for anybody to realize you. [She looks toward the Stage Manager and asks abruptly, through her tears] Do any human beings ever realize life while they live it?—every, every minute?

Stage Manager: No. [Pause] The saints and poets, maybe—they do some." [17]

My concocting and writing this book about death has sharpened my appreciation of life also—beyond all my expectations. The thought of death has made my life exactly the opposite of "morbid." But why passively read about this experience in other people? Why not actively enact it in yourself, right now, this very minute? "Look thy last on all things lovely" now. You have something infinitely better to do than to continue reading this book. Meet your friend. Lay the book down for ten minutes and ask yourself what you would think, feel, say, and do if you knew this was the last ten minutes of your life. And then do it. For the very good reason that it might really *be* the last ten minutes of your life, and for the equally good reason that some ten minutes quite certainly *will* be the last.

Are you back? Don't rush. Relish. Let it work.

How does it work? Why does death enhance life? Because it makes life scarce, and scarcity confers value. Why is "September Song" so poignant? Because of its sense of "these few precious days"—precious *because few*. A seventeenth-century "September Song," Andrew Marvell's "To His Coy Mistress," has the same poignancy and the same reason for it: death. "Had we but world enough and time," says the poet, he would spend centuries admiring each of her features:

But at my back I always hear
Time's winged chariot hurrying near;
And yonder all before us lie
Deserts of vast eternity. [18]

Death especially confers value on love. In Heinlein's *Time Enough for Love,* the classic fairy-tale motif of the immortal elf-maiden falling in love with a mortal man and thus with her doom, is transposed into a science-fiction framework. An immortal from another planet, who has loved millions of immortals, falls in love with an earth woman. Because of her mortality, he knows true love for the first time. Without death, there could be no love.

What would be valuable, what would be appreciated, if it were not for death? Not love, not time, not anything. The true value of anything in life, and of life itself, is revealed most clearly by its absence, its death; for example:

—any little thing you take for granted, like electricity during a power failure;

—the wilderness: when it abounded, we took it for granted; now that it is scarce, we begin to appreciate it;

—a separated lover, of whom "absence makes the heart grow fonder";

—your lost youth, or health, or freedom from pain, disease, or imprisonment, appreciated only when it is gone;

—a friend, parent, child, or anyone you love or admire, who "leaves an empty spot against the sky" when he dies;

—God: what difference does it make whether there is a God or not? Read the great atheists like Sartre, Camus, Nietzsche, Beckett, and Bertrand Russell to find out. The silhouette drawn by God's absence in such writers is sharper than the one drawn by His presence in most believers.

—life itself: how precious was your life and your world to you during the ten minutes when you imagined you were about to lose it forever? And that was only imagination; what would the real thing be?

My daughter was never more precious to me than when the doctor diagnosed in her an apparently malignant brain tumor. (The diagnosis was wrong, but she will always be specially precious to me because of this experience.) See the appendix.

Death as well as life is appreciated most when threatened. Not only does death frame life, it also frames itself! The value of life is appreciated best when it is threatened by death; the value of death is appreciated best when it is threatened by the death of death in the form of the "immortality pill." (See the section "Openness," page 41.) The test of the meaning of anything, says William James, is the answer to the question "What difference does it make?"[19] Suppose there were no death. What difference would it make? Kill death and you will know the value of this friend. You will miss him when he is gone.

Also, just as the realization of death's imminence allows us to appreciate life, so the realization of the imminence of old age allows us to appreciate life, especially the life of youth and middle age. From youth's point of view, middle age appears as a loss, a diminution to be lamented; but from old age's point of view, it appears as a gift to be appreciat-

ed. Remember that a glass filled halfway with water is called half empty if you take for granted its fullness, half full if you do not. Youth
takes for granted life and health, and is therefore offended at the half
empty cup of days that is middle age and the nearly empty cup that is
old age. "Youth is wasted on the young." Youth lives forward, from
past to future; its past and present health is the beginning, the assumed
point of view, the taken-for-granted standpoint in assessing middle age
and aging. Middle age teaches us the great lesson of living backwards,
from the future, out of old age and death, appreciating both the life
that is gone and the life that is left, noticing the half *full* cup with eyes
that do not take for granted fullness and life and health. Without death
there would not be gratitude for life.

I know of a woman whose husband died in the prime of life at age
41. When she knew he was dead, she said, with a voice full of wonder,
"Forty-one wonderful years!" She had learned the secret. She knew
how to live backwards. Death is our friend because it teaches us that
secret.

DEATH AS FOOD

A fifth reason why death is a friend is that death is our food. Death
does not eat us; we eat death. Death is like matter, mystery, and time in
that all four are digestible raw material for the human spirit. All four
can be threatening to it, like a block of marble to a sculptor uncertain
of his talents, or the boxing ring to a loser; *or* they can be inviting and
fulfilling if they are matter conquered, used, in-formed, transformed,
assimilated, digested. Let us see how each of these four things is our
food.

Without matter, there is nothing for our spirit to use to express itself, to relate to other spirits, to meet in. Matter is like a street corner;
spirit is like the people who meet there.

Without mystery, there is nothing for mind to digest. Mind does not
conquer or eliminate mystery; it digests it and transforms it into understanding, as a human body transforms a roast duck into living human
tissue. If mind simply destroyed mystery, it would have nothing to feed
on, nothing to explore. It would starve. When there is no unknown,
there is no known. The known does not replace the unknown as a new
car replaces an old car, but rather as an adult "replaces" a child. The
unknown *becomes* known; the child becomes the adult; but the old car

does not become the new car (in fact, the new car becomes the old car).

Without time, our mind has no food either. The mind has a more-than-temporal dimension to it, but this dimension needs time as its food. The more-than-temporal dimension can be shown to exist by noticing that the mind can calculate and relate different moments of time, different nows. In order to do this, it must have a vantage point superior to time, just as in order to calculate and relate different two-dimensional shapes on the flat ground we must move above the ground through the third dimension. For the same reason, there is something infinite about the mind's ability to calculate and relate different finite numbers in a number series. The knower must always be more than the objects known.

But this transtemporal dimension of the mind would be empty of content if it did not have a temporal world to know. Time is the food of a more-than-temporal mind, the raw material.

Similarly, death is the material continually digested by life. We think of death as eating up and destroying life; but it is life that eats death without destroying it. It is life's nourishment. Life's best wine is served last. Without death, there could be no life for us, just as without death there could be no self. (See the section "A Frame for Life" on page 43.) Our life *is* only because it is a continuous victory over its non-being, over death. Life means that we do not fall, though we are suspended over nothingness. Without that suspense, we could not be said to be victors over falling. Just as "staying up" is meaningless without a "down" to fall into, so life is meaningless unless there is death.

Our life, unlike that of an angel, is not a static, secure, timeless fact, but a dynamic, dramatic, dangerous achievement, a series of moment-by-moment, continuous leaps over the abyss of death. We *can* die at any moment—unlike an angel—but we don't—*also unlike an angel*. Our life is the continual conquest of a real possibility, of death. Life is like a pearl: it needs a grain of sand at its center—death—as the irritant, the enemy, to stimulate the production of the mother-of-pearl of life around it. But death remains at its center. At the heart of life there is death. Death is our being. Man *is* mortal.

DEATH AND TRUTH

A sixth reason why death is a friend sounds even stranger than calling death food (but much of what we are finding out about death sounds strange). *Without death there could be no truth.*

This is connected with two similar strange discoveries: (1) that without death there could be no self, and (2) that without death there could be no life. I mean by "truth" *lived* truth, the truth of being a true self. It is what the Old Testament Hebrews called *emeth* and the existentialists called "authenticity." This truth is not just known but "be-ed," existed, lived. It comes only as a lived answer to a lived quest, not a thought answer to a thought question. A quest is not merely a question. The intellect asks a question; a whole person lives a quest. *Emeth* is found by questing, not just by questioning. It is the kind of truth that can only be found with the whole of one's being—the kind of Truth Socrates and Buddha found. Of *this* truth Jesus says, "The one who searches always finds."[20] The hard thing here is not to find but to seek. For such a seeking requires "a leap through which man thrusts away all the previous security, whether real or imagined, of his life."[21] It is like Abraham dying to the security of Ur, Peter dying to the security of his boat; it is stepping out into the unknown. To ask such a question, to go on such a quest, is not merely to repeat an interrogative formula; it is to *raise* the question from death to life, to create it anew, and to feel its being, its weight, its strength. Indeed, to ask a question in this way is the most creative thing a human being can do; it is to *create* in the true sense of the word—to make not out of previously existing materials in the environment, but to make out of your own inner power something that simply was not there before. This is truly godlike, and the clearest distinction between a human mind and a computer. Computers do not create. They do not question.

For me to find this kind of truth, it must become a matter of life or death. Truth must mean more to me than life, and ignorance of it more than death. Four examples of this attitude are Socrates, Buddha, St. Augustine, and Kierkegaard. All were single-minded, not double-minded. Their wills were like laser beams, narrow and powerful and pure. "Purity of Heart," as Kierkegaard reminds us, "is to will one thing."[22] That one thing for these men was truth.

Facing death by execution, Socrates makes his greatest statement of the truth about truth-seeking. In reading the following statement, remember that wickedness is equated with ignorance, virtue with truth:

> The difficult thing is not to escape death, I think, but to escape wickedness—that is much more difficult, for that runs faster than death. And now

I, being slow and old, have been caught . by the slower one; but my accusers, being clever and quick, have been caught by the swifter, badness. And now I and they depart, I, condemned by you to death, but these, condemned by truth to depravity and injustice. I abide by my penalty, they by theirs.[23]

Kierkegaard is an admirer of Socrates's single-mindedness: "Our philosophers have many thoughts, all valid to a certain extent; Socrates, had only one, which was absolute."[24] Therefore, Kierkegaard has the truth-seeker say to the pleasure-seeker:

> One is not tempted to pity you but rather to wish that some day the circumstances of your life may tighten upon you the screws in its rack and compel you to come out with what really dwells in you; that they may begin the sharper inquisition of the rack which cannot be beguiled by nonsense and witticisms. . . . Do you not know that there comes a midnight hour when every one has to throw off his mask? Do you believe you can slip away a little before midnight in order to avoid this? Or are you not terrified by it? I have seen men in real life who so long deceived others that at last their true nature could not reveal itself. . . . Or can you think of anything more frightful than that it might end with your nature being resolved into a multiplicity, that you really might become many, become, like those unhappy demoniacs, a legion, and you thus would have lost the inmost and holiest thing of all in a man, the unifying power of personality?[25]

The "midnight hour when every one has to throw off his mask" is death. (Even the Cinderella story is about death!) Kierkegaard is here painting a picture of Hell. This Hell is not external and geographical but internal; it is a state of consciousness, or nonconsciousness: "In fact you are nothing; you are merely a relation to others."[26] If I am nothing but a relation to others, then there is nobody *there* when I remove my masks; there *is* no I to survive death. We recognize the picture as terrifyingly familiar, a universal fear, a primal nightmare, the picture of The Man with No Face.[27] We avoid it by avoidng any thought of "the midnight hour when every one has to throw off his mask." The midnight hour is really our friend because it elicits from us the truth of our selves. And truth is what Heaven is made of.

St. Augustine's incredible honesty and intolerance of even the slightest self-deception in his *Confessions* also comes from his realization of death:

> Such thoughts I revolved in my unhappy heart, which was further burdened and gnawed at by the fear that I should die without having found the truth.[28]

Buddha preaches his famous "Arrow Sermon"[29] in answer to Malunkyaputta, a disciple who seeks truths instead of truth. Malunkyaputta wants Buddha to satisfy his philosophical curiosity on many things, but Buddha teaches only One Thing. He says to Malunkyaputta: Suppose you were shot with a poisoned arrow and a doctor offered to take it out; would you first demand that he answer questions like: Who shot it? What clan was he from? What was his motive? What did he make the arrow out of? and many other questions?—if so, *you would die* before the arrow was out. Finding the one thing necessary, *Emeth,* the truth, is a matter of life and death.

Only because there is death can there be truth. To will truth as one thing, one must be one person, of one mind and will; but to be one person, one must be mortal. Death strips off the many, the masks; the naked one, the true self, lives because of death.

The *approach* of death in old age also brings this oneness, as if death were breathing onto life from ahead. Think of three stages: first, the nonbeing that precedes birth; second, life; third, the death that follows life. Within the second stage, life, there are also three stages recapitulating the same pattern: being born, living, and dying. And within the second of *these* three stages, living, there are also three stages: youth, maturity, and old age. In each of the three three-stage processes, there is first a simplicity, then a complexity, then a simplicity again, as death brings the final simplification. The young are simple and single-hearted. As we mature, we lose that Eden; we learn that "life's just not that simple." But when we are old, we can distill our life's wisdom into simplicity. St. Paul distills the whole meaning of his life into one word when he writes to the Phillipians that "for me to live is Christ, and to die is gain."[30]

The infant and the old man are simple because they are both near eternity, which is simple, like a point. Time is like a line, and death is like the last point on the line—or rather, the whole line looked at end-on, as a point. Life is complex; death is simple. We need both friends.

DEATH AND HEROISM

A seventh reason death is a friend is that it makes heroism possible. By heroism I mean not just courage but greatness, bigness of spirit, significance. This point is powerfully put in Ernst Becker's *The Denial of Death*.[31] The kind of flat, dull egalitarianism Nietzsche so despised as sheepish and fit for "the last man" who has "invented happiness" and "blinks"—this cannot face death. The thought of death is the death of "the last man." For death is an extreme, the last extremity; and "the last man" fears all extremes, therefore refuses heroism.

But in the light of death, everything takes on extreme value to us, and every choice takes on extreme and heroic importance. Sartre discovered this in a Gestapo prison, and it is one of the few heroic notes in an otherwise notably unheroic philosopher:

> We were never more free than during the German occupation. We had lost all our rights, beginning with the right to talk. Every day we were insulted to our faces and had to take it in silence. Under one pretext or another, as workers, Jews, or political prisoners, we were deported en masse. Everywhere, on billboards, in the newspapers, on the screen, we encountered the revolting and insipid picture of ourselves that our suppressors wanted us to accept. And because of all this we were free. Because the Nazi venom seeped into our thoughts, every accurate thought was a conquest. Because an all-powerful police tried to force us to hold our tongues, every word took on the value of a declaration of principles. Because we were hunted down, every one of our gestures had the weight of a solemn commitment. . . .
>
> Exile, captivity, and especially death (which we usually shrink from facing at all in happier days) became for us the habitual objects of our concern. We learned that they were neither inevitable accidents, nor even constant and inevitable dangers, but they must be considered as our lot itself, our destiny, the profound source of our reality as men. At every instant we lived up to the full sense of this commonplace little phrase: "Man is mortal!" And the choice that each of us made of his life was an authentic choice because it was made face to face with death, because it could always have been expressed in these terms: "Rather death than . . ."[32]

Death teaches both resolution and detachment, teaches us "to care and not to care":[33] to care resolutely for all that is important and detachedly not to care for all that is unimportant. Death teaches us to live on the heroic heights by bringing us into the depths; for the heights are measured by the depths.

FRIEND OR ENEMY? AN UNRESOLVED RIDDLE

Death, then, is a friend. To see death as a friend is better than to see death as a stranger. But it is still not enough. Why? Why must we explore further? Most current books on death do not.

It is true, as such books say, that making death a stranger, repressing the knowledge of death, has made life empty and meaningless. But does merely facing death make life full and meaningful? It makes it honest. But honesty is not yet meaningfulness, only its necessary precondition, as sincerity is not yet virtue but only the necessary precondition for all virtue. In both cases, modern man tends to judge the precondition alone sufficient, because it's much easier.

Facing death does not in itself solve the problem of death any more than facing cancer cures cancer. But we cannot cure it without facing it. It is necessary but not sufficient.

It is especially not sufficient to dispel the guilt about death that we discovered toward the end of Chapter 1. The imperative to face death in fact only increases our guilt, for it is another imperative that we are guilty of disobeying, thus another reason for feeling guilty. Who is as honest toward death as he ought to be? The problem is the same as that in an ethic of mere forgiveness—in seeking to dispel guilt, it gives us one more thing to feel guilty about, for who is as forgiving as he ought to be? Our nonforgivingness is one of the things for which we need to be forgiven. We need something more.

A great paradox has emerged from our exploration of the relation between death and truth, between death and the self, between death and the truth of the self, *emeth*. It is that on the one hand, "If there were no Death, there could be no Truth."[34] Death is a friend to truth and self. On the other hand, "What truth can there be if there is death?"[35] Death is both our friend and our enemy.

We said earlier that the paradox is tolerable if death is like a sparring partner: It is our enemy *because* it is our friend. As a friend, it is performing a necessary role for us, the role of enemy. But this is not enough. Sparring partners are not supposed to kill you, only toughen you up. Suffering can be seen as a sparring partner, but not death. For death does not, it seems, toughen the self but rather weakens it to the point of extinction.

So we have not yet resolved our paradox. Our discovery of death as a friend does not yet answer the problems we found in our discovery of death as an enemy; it only adds to them, creating a contradictory half of the picture, a paradox, not a resolution. On the one hand, death is loss of self; on the other, loss of death is loss of meaning, of identity, of self. On the one hand, death takes from me my self, and immortality would give me my self snatched from the jaws of death, the jaws of nothingness. On the other hand, death gives me my self, as we have discovered in this chapter, and the "immortality pill" would snatch it from me. Death both unmakes me and makes me.

To unravel this riddle of death as enemy and death as friend we must go beyond death as enemy and death as friend. There are two human relationships in which friendship and enmity, love and hate, often coexist with great effect: the relation between parent (especially mother) and child, and the romantic relationship, the relationship between two lovers. Let us explore these two deeper faces of death.

NOTES

1. Martin Heidegger, *Being and Time* (New York: Harper & Row, 1962), p. 296.
2. *Book of Common Prayer,* Burial Service. Bartlett [*Familiar Quotations* (Boston: Little, Brown, 1897), p. 851] says: "This is derived from a Latin antiphon, said to have been composed by Notker, a monk of St. Gall, in 911, while watching somewourkmen building a bridge at Martinsbrüke, in peril of their lives. It forms the groundwork of Luther's antiphon 'De Morte.' "
3. Aristotle, *Nicomachean Ethics,* trans. Martin Ostwald (Indianapolis: Bobbs-Merrill, 1962), p. 253.
4. See C. S. Lewis, *The Four Loves* (London: Collins Fontana Books, 1960), p. 58: "Lovers are normally face to face, absorbed in each other; Friends, side by side, absorbed in some common interest."
5. A line from "Suicide is Painless," the theme song of *M.A.S.H.* Music by Johnny Mandel, lyrics by Mike Altman, 1968.
6. Plato *Phaedo* 64a.
7. Cor. 13:8–10; Heb. 12:26–29.
8. Heidegger, *Being and Time,* p. 281.
9. Sheldon Vanauken, *A Severe Mercy* (San Francisco: Harper & Row, 1977), pp. 185, 195.
10. Max Picard, *The World of Silence* (Chicago: Regnery, 1952), p. 232.
11. Walter de la Mare, "Fare Well," in *The Complete Poems of Walter de la Mare* (London: Faber & Faber, 1968), p. 218.
12. C.S. Lewis, *Miracles* (New York: Macmillan, 1955), pp. 80–81.
13. Nikos Kazantzakis, *The Odyssey, A Modern Sequel,* trans. Kimon Friar (New York: Simon & Schuster, 1958), bk. 18, p. 912.
14. Picard, *World of Silence,* pp. 217–218.
15. Viktor Frankl, "Basic Concepts of Logotherapy," *Journal of Existential Psychiatry* 3 (1962), pp. 111–118.
16. James L. Christian, *Philosophy, An Introduction to the Art of Wondering* (San Francisco: Rinehart Press, 1973), pp. 10–11.
17. Thornton Wilder, *Our Town* (New York: Coward-McCann, 1938; Harper, 1957), pp. 124–125, 127–128.
18. Andrew Marvell, "To His Coy Mistress." in *The Poems of Andrew Marvell,* ed. J. Reeves & M. Seymour-Smith (New York: Barnes & Noble, 1969).

19. William James, "Preface to the Meaning of Truth," in *Pragmatism and Other Essays*, p. 135. See also p. 66.
20. Matt. 7:7 (Jerusalem Bible).
21. Martin Heidegger, *Introduction to Metaphysics* (New York: Doubleday Anchor, 1964), p. 5.
22. Søren Kierkegaard, *Purity of Heart*, trans. Douglas V. Steere (New York: Harper, 1938).
23. Plato *Apology of Socrates* 40b.
24. Søren Kierkegaard, *Philosophical Fragments*, trans. David Swenson and Howard V. Hong (Princeton, N.J.: Princeton University Press, 1967), p. 12, n. 2. The text reads: "Such is the criticism commonly passed upon Socrates in our age [that 'his thought "had no positive content" '], which boasts of its positivity much as if a polytheist were to speak with scorn of the negativity of a monotheist, for the polytheist has many gods, the monotheist only one. So our philosophers have many thoughts, all valid to a certain extent; Socrates had only one, which was absolute."
25. Søren Kierkegaard, *Either/Or*, vol. 2, *Equilibrium* in *A Kierkegaard Anthology*, ed. Robert Bretall (Princeton, N.J.: Princeton University Press, 1936), pp. 99–100.
26. Ibid.
27. Two contemporary novelistic treatments of this primal nightmare occur in Alfred Bester's *The Demolished Man* (New York: Garland Pub., 1975) and J. R. R. Tolkien's *The Lord of the Rings*, vol. 3, *The Return of the King* (Boston: Houghton Mifflin, 1965).
28. Augustine *Confessions* 7. 5.
29. See E. A. Burtt, *The Teachings of the Compassionate Buddha* (New York: Mentor Books, 1955), "Questions Not Tending to Edification," pp. 32–36.
30. Phil. 1:21.
31. Ernst Becker, *The Denial of Death* (New York: Macmillan, Free Press, 1973).
32. From "The Republic of Silence." Quoted by William Barrett in *Irrational Man* (New York: Doubleday Anchor Books, 1962), pp. 239–240.
33. T. S. Eliot, "Ash Wednesday," in *Collected Poems* (New York: Harcourt, Brace & World, 1963).
34. p. 52.
35. From Tolstoy, "The Death of Ivan Ilyitch." Quoted in Barrett, *Irrational Man*, p. 145.

CHAPTER 4

Death as a Mother

Mother is a relative term. Mothers are mothers in relation to children, as children are children in relation to mothers. What a mother is *to a child* is therefore part of her essence as a mother.

What, then, is a mother to a child? A place. To a child a mother is a place, like a womb, both before and after birth. "Mother" means "home": the center of the cosmos, the navel of the earth, the sacred space. Primitive tribes, especially those close to "Mother Earth," often erect their temple or sacred tent at the place believed to be the geographical center of the earth, with the tent pole sticking umbilically into 'the earth's navel'.[1] To a child, a mother is such a temple. She escapes Einsteinian relativity; she constitutes an absolute point of reference in space. This is why children love fat mothers: They are more obviously *places;* they seem more *put,* more placed, more like the earth itself.

Their simple instinct to see mother as a place is accurate; for what makes a mother a mother, literally and physiologically, is precisely a space, a hole. A mother is a birth canal, or a structure of flesh surrounding a birth canal: life surrounding life. She gathers, surrounds, and makes concave shapes because her body is itself a gathering, a surrounding, a concavity.[2]

(A *woman* is not essentially a birth canal, because a woman is not *essentially* a mother. For nothing can ever not be what it essentially is, and a woman can obviously be a woman without being a mother.)

DOORS

A mother, then, is essentially a canal (at least from a biological point of view). Now a birth canal is a door—a magic door, in fact, not merely a door from one part of the world to another part, but a door from one whole world to another. Fairy tales are full of such magic doors or passages, for fairy tales are expressions of our deep, unconscious longings, loves, and wonderings, and few things are more wonderful than a door into another world. Imagine how you would feel if you discovered such a door in the so-called real world!

Children love doors, for doors can be either open or closed; thus they fulfill two great needs of the human spirit: the need for mystery and for exploration. The two alternatives to a door are a wall and a space, mere closedness or mere openness. Neither is as wonderful as a door. Children, like adults, hate enclosing walls, for they signify confinement and frustration. Claustrophobia is latent in everyone. But children, unlike many adults, also hate doorless, roomless, open houses where every room is open to and flows into every other room and everything lies naked and open to view at once, for such a modern interior design expresses the loss of mystery, like the larger modern world outside. There is efficiency but no surprises. Children love to explore houses with secret panels, hidden staircases, and so on. They love to make hiding places such as tents, forts, or little enclosures; for these promise surprises, secrets, mysteries.

So does a door. A door offers the best of both worlds, both mystery (when closed) and the exploration of mystery (when opened). But a door must be not just open but opened; an open door that was closed until just now is much more exciting than an open door that was always open. A door that is never open is frustrating; a door that is never closed is boring. (The dilemma of boredom vs. frustration is far more profound than it seems. It plunges us directly into the greatest question, the question of happiness, the question of heaven. How can there be a happiness which is neither boring—if the end is attained— nor frustrating—if it isn't?)

A sacrament is also a door, and not an ordinary door but a magic door; not a door from one part of the world to another, but a door to and from another world—like a birth canal. (This is part of the meaning of the concept "sacrament." Whether a sacrament is true, whether it really "works," is a matter of faith, but what "sacrament" means is a matter of definition.) The "other world" into which a sacramental door opens is the world of the supernatural, the world of God.

A sacrament is thus a miracle. The word that is usually translated as "miracle" in the New Testament really means "sign."[3] The miracles of Jesus were called signs; they were interpreted by his disciples not simply as power displays but as signs from His Father, little liftings of the curtain between man and God that had fallen in Eden, little peepholes through which man could see what God was like and what God was doing (healing, enlightening, and so on). Some of the ancient Greeks thought the stars were miracles in this sense, peepholes in the dark curtain of the night through which man could glimpse the light of the gods.

The New Testament calls Jesus "the Word of God,"[4] the expression or manifestation of God, the window or peephole through which man can see God, the sign ("miracle") of God. Jesus also says: "I am the door."[5] A door is even more than a window; for a window is only to see through, while a door is to go through. Protestants believe sacraments are like windows, that is, signs, symbols. Catholics believe sacraments are like doors, that is, that actual transactions are carried on "ex opere operato"[6] by them and not just by their users. A sacrament is thus defined in Catholic doctrine as a sign that effects what it signifies.[7] Protestants too see Jesus as a sacrament in the Catholic sense, not just in the Protestant sense. He actually effects transaction between man and God, the exchange of grace for sin, eternal life for eternal death, God's heaven for man's hell. The cross is the place of this interchange, the cosmic door, the primary sacrament of all human history. In the Christian story, Jesus' death opened the door between Heaven and Earth. The veil in the temple was torn in two at the moment Jesus died.[8] This veil separated the Holy of Holies from the rest of the world. This holiest place symbolized the dwelling of God. Thus Jesus' death opened the door between two worlds. This is also why "the bodies of many holy men rose from the dead" at the same time[9]—they were travellers through the newly opened door, the door of death.

DEATH AS A DOOR

All death is a door. Jesus' death, for a Christian, is a special door. All death is a sacrament, the primary sacrament in every person's life.

Jesus' death, for a Christian, energizes these other deaths, opens the door of death, wins through to heaven for man, transforms death from a hole into a door, from a door to nonbeing into a door to being, from a door to hell into a door to heaven. The early Christians called the day of their death *dies natalis,* birthday.

A door has two sides. So does death. We saw in Chapter 1 that death is not merely a part of this world, not merely a natural event. Another person's death is a part of the world to me (though not to him), but mine is not. A door between two worlds is not merely a part of either of these worlds. It is that fascinating thing, a boundary, an edge, an absolute. My own death appears as such an absolute, as an emptiness, as "the jaws of nothingness." But an emptiness may be either a hole or a door, either a bottomless pit or a passageway, either a tunnel opening to nowhere or a tunnel opening to somewhere, some other world . . . like a birth canal.

If death is like a birth canal, then life comes out of death, fullness out of emptiness, as a baby comes out of the birth canal. Perhaps this is one of the deeper meanings of Sampson's mysterious riddle. Sampson found sweet honey in a dead lion's rotting carcass, and formulated the riddle "Out of the strong came forth sweetness; out of the eater came forth the eaten."[10] Death is like that lion: strong, an eater of men, and a rotting corpse. If death is like a birth canal, then out of it also comes the sweetest honey of life.

A Christian would see an even more specific and striking meaning in Sampson's riddle. Eternal life comes out of a cross of death. Man finds God—where? There, where the terrible cry goes up: "My God, my God, why hast Thou forsaken me?"[11]

A THOUGHT EXPERIMENT: DEATH AS BIRTH

Let us make another thought experiment. Let us suppose that death is indeed a door, not a hole; a birth canal, not a bottomless pit; a mother giving life, not a spider sucking it away. Let us suppose that dying is a kind of being born; let us suppose that this most suggestive image of the world's greatest poets, this commonest belief of the world's greatest religions, and this profoundest thought of the world's greatest philosophers[12] is true. Let us make the daring and paradoxical supposition that our wise men are really wise. Let us not yet *believe,* only *suppose,* as a thought experiment. Let us gaze at this picture a while before deciding whether to buy it; let us finger this jewel, heft it, explore it, shine many-angled lights on it, before deciding whether it is an authentic diamond or a man-made imitation. Let us explore the landscape of death as a mother.

LITTLE DEATHS

A first consequence of our thought experiment is that if it is true, it fits in with and makes sense of a most pervasive feature of our lives; that is, throughout our lives, death and birth repeat themselves. Many little deaths lead to many little births. We die to wombs and are born into worlds. But these worlds become larger wombs for us. We die to them and are born into larger worlds: our mother's womb, the breast, the nursery, the home, neighborhood, family, school, each grade in school, friends, jobs, cities. We are like multistage rockets; each stage dies and falls away when its job is done, for its job is only to launch us forward.

Death is the mystery present in all of life:

> The mystery which was supposed to be at work in the life of Israel
> . . . and which was made present to them in the rite of the Tabernacle, was
> the mystery upon which all life proceeds and which will never be outgrown
> since it is there at the root of all things. It is the mystery of My Life For
> Yours. It is expressed in the words "I owe my life to you, and I lay down my
> life for you."
>
> No one has ever drawn a single breath on any other basis. No child has
> ever received life to begin with without a "laying down" of life by the two
> people to whom he owes his conception, and by the laying down of his mother's life for months in bearing and nourishing him. . . . And no one has ever
> sat down to the smallest pittance of food that he did not owe to somebody's
> life having been laid down, if it was only a prawn or a lettuce leaf. . .[13]

The multistage rockets that we are include not only ourselves but others; in fact, they include the whole cosmos. Stars, dinosaurs, and spermatozoa must die for us to be born; the principle of the co-inherence of life and death works both before and after our birth. As worlds had to die for us to be born, so we must die to worlds after worlds once we are born.

If all of life is a series of little births through little deaths, it seems to be a clue (though not a *proof*) that birth and death as such always imply and contain each other; that just as our birth is the beginning of our dying (as soon as we are born, we begin to die), so also our death is the beginning of our being born: Death is our mother.

Let us explore more of the similarities between death and birth, more of the brush strokes in the portrait of death as a mother.

THE PROCESS OF DYING/BEING BORN

The process of being born looks like the process of dying. Labor and delivery is the most radical and rapid change a human body ever experiences. We are thrust violently out of a comfortable, homey, confining place. We seem to fight for air as we are forcibly expelled from our old body, the womb. In the womb, we were not clearly conscious of our body as distinct from the womb; the whole womb *was* our body. Now that we are being expelled from it, it seems as if we are being expelled from our body, rather than being born into our body. Just so, when we die, it seems as if we are separated from the body, not that our true body is then born.

The place into which we are thrust does not appear as home but as "unhomely," *unheimlich,* uncanny, terrifying, the great unknown behind the door. Yet it is in fact our truer home, just as the earth is more ours than the womb, which is not *our* womb but our mother's womb. We have only tenanted it; it was ours only on loan. So the world after death is more ours than this world, which is only tenanted, rented from Mother Earth for a while.

Yet even though there is a terror of this new "unhomely home," there is also a natural drive or desire, a purposive movement toward it, toward this unknown goal. We perceive this drive from without, objectively, in the case of the fetus, as a biological fact; but we do not know whether the fetus experiences the drive within itself, subjectively, as a desire or longing to be born. But we do experience the subjective, inner desire or longing in this world for something more, for the ideal, for heaven, for truth and goodness and beauty, for perfect freedom and "the peace which the world cannot give."[14] This is the "restless heart,"[15] the "divine discontent,"[16] the "Is That All There Is?" "Thou hast made everything beautiful (fitting) in its time," says Ecclesiastes, but "also Thou hast put eternity into his heart,"[17] the seat of the desires. While we can observe the objective goal but not the subjective desire for it in the case of the fetus, we can observe the subjective desire but not the objective goal in our own case. Unless we are told by some word from another world, by some outside observer who stands to us as we stand to a fetus, we do not know from our experience of this world alone whether or not death is a birth and the fulfillment of our deepest desire, just as the fetus cannot know (as we objective observers can) whether birth is its fulfillment, until it happens. "Under the sun," says Ecclesiastes, "who knows if the soul of man goes upward while the soul of the beast returns into the earth?" [18] Unless we are told by some word from another world—but that word can be accepted only by faith, by trust in the report based on trust in the reporter. It cannot be proved by worldly experience and reason; the camera without its own inner flash bulb of faith to cast additional light on the world can take only available-light exposures, and the available light from the world is riddling and uncertain. Nevertheless, it is full of hints, shadows that seem to point to substance: parallels, analogies, likenesses that amount to likelihoods. Perhaps it is not enough for faith, but it is enough for hope.

We may hope beyond appearances because appearances do not reveal all. We see only dying; we do not see death. Within the process of being born, birth pains are not yet birth, and do not reveal to the fetus the true meaning of birth. So death pains and the process of dying are not yet death, and do not reveal to the dying person the true meaning of death. If death is a door, as our thought experiment has supposed, it has two sides, as the sea has two shores. We see only one, the less important one: the common departure from the familiar place, not the various arrivals at the new one. All the ships depart from the same shore and seem to pass into the same nothingness—we seem to be all the same and all extinguished in death—yet ships arrive at different ports; neither their existence nor their uniqueness is extinguished.

RETURNEES FROM DEATH?

When a few people do seem to catch a glimpse of the other shore, whether through mystical experience or through medical death (or near death) and resuscitation, it is only a distant glimpse; it is a vision of another country from afar, not a living in it. (In fact, since they return, it is *not* an experience of true death, since death is essentially irreversible, nonreturnable, a one-way trip. No one has simply returned from death. Even Jesus did not return to his mortal body but resurrected to his immortal body.) One feature reported by all such travellers is the ineffability of the experience: "Words can't describe it."[19] For language is the horizon of meaning, or at least of communication; and at death the ship of self passes under that horizon.

Shortly after birth, how much does a baby know of this world? About that much, or less, in our analogy, do such travellers in the country of death know of life in the next world. We should probably take their accounts seriously, but only as we should take the account of a baby. The death-traveller, like the birth-traveller, is a neophyte; he cannot comprehend his new world at first any more than a newborn baby can. There is indescribably more to it.

Yet they say something. Their experience of life after death is not so utterly different from life before death that absolutely nothing can be communicated about it. Their words are not random nonsense, but meaningful symbols, pictures, hints, or shadows.

There are three possibilities for any word's meaning. A word can be used univocally, equivocally, or analogically. A word used univocally always has the same, literal, clearly definable meaning. A word used equivocally has two completely different meanings, which are unrelated, so that from one use of the word we cannot know anything about the other (for example, the bark of a dog and the bark of a tree). A word used analogically has two different but related meanings (for example, "I see" with my eyes and "I see" with my mind).

Now if the two worlds, the world before death and the world after death, are the same, then words describing the world after death will have the same meaning they do when used to describe this world. They will be univocal. If the two worlds are wholly different, all words describing them will be equivocal, and there can be no communication at all of the other world to us in this world. But if the worlds are different but related, then words describing them will be analogical.

And if the worlds are related by image—that is, if this world is an image, sign, picture, symbol, shadow, or likeness of another—then words describing this world are shadows or symbols or likenesses of the other world. It seems at first that this-worldly words are literal and other-worldly words are symbolic, but it must be the other way round. If this whole world is an image of another, then everything in this world shares in that image-status, and language about everything in this world is imagery in relation to the other world. The mystics' language is not symbolic but literal; it is our language that is symbolic. For instance, when a mystic or a resuscitated patient reports an inward vision of spiritual light, he is *not* borrowing from our sense experience of physical light to make a metaphor; it is the physical light, and the word that designates it, that is the metaphor.

If our parallel between birth and death is sound, the same relationship holds true between earth language and heaven language as between womb language and earth language. Imagine a little fetus; here it is, ejected from the womb, travelling the great journey down the birth canal; now it plops out into the world. It seems to be born. But its umbilical cord is not yet cut; therefore it is not yet born, not *irreversibly* born. Through an extremely unusual feat of medical technology, it might be returned to the womb. Just so, a dying patient who seems, both to himself and to others, to have died, but is then resuscitated, has not died—not *irreversibly* died. He has not crossed "the border."[20] Now suppose this fetus, somehow put back into the womb, tells another fetus about "life after birth." (Suppose there is a fetus language and communication, for the sake of the story and its parallelism.) It would use such words as *life* or *pleasure* or *consciousness* to describe life outside the womb. Such words would mean something *like* fetus life, fetus pleasure, and fetus consciousness, but also something vastly different. Such words would be used analogically. Just so does our present language use words like *bliss, vision, union,* and so forth to describe life after death. These words are meaningful symbols, pointers down an infinite corridor; they can point our thought in the right direction, but they cannot carry it to its end.

LIFE AS FETAL REHEARSALS

In the womb, the fetus practices many of the acts it will need to perform once it is born, such as kicking and swallowing. Similarly, in the world, a person practices the acts he or she will need to perform after death, especially knowing and loving, the two values emphasized by all the saints, mystics, wise men, and resuscitated patients.

Some of the physical habits the fetus learns in the womb are necessary for its survival both in the womb and in the world, such as heartbeat. Others make sense only in the world outside the womb, such as kicking. These are essentially preparatory acts, rehearsals. So in our analogy, some of the spiritual habits or virtues that we learn in this life are necessary to our survival in the world, such as justice and wisdom; but others do not seem to make rational, this-worldly sense: virtues like humility, martyrdom, or the "divine discontent," the longing for perfection. The specifically Christian virtues taught in the Gospels are absurd to the world, even the wise world. Contrast the ethics of Aristotle with the ethics of the New Testament! Poverty, chastity, and obedience make no sense if this world is all there is. They limit the this-worldly me; they repress my desire for this-worldly gratification and pleasure. They seem to be weaknesses, not strengths. Indeed, this is probably *the* most popular criticism of Christian ethics, both among playboys and practical people, and among psychologists and philosophers like Freud, Sartre, Nietzsche, and Marx. But if this world is a womb, Christian values do make sense as training for the next world. Jesus preaches his ethic as an ethic of the New Kingdom, the "Kingdom of Heaven." A fetus might wonder what his feet are for, might wonder where in the womb he will find them useful and fulfilling; but the womb gives him no adequate answer. Similarly, the world gives me no adequate answer when I wonder what such things as self-sacrifice or my longing for eternal joy mean.

Therefore, the attempt to teach traditional Christian values such as idealism and self-sacrifice without the vision of a life after death ultimately makes no sense, and is quickly detected as senseless by young, critical minds. Lip service may be paid to this ethic, but it is ignored in practice; or else its claws are pulled and it is reinterpreted in reasonable this-worldly terms, such as: if you have self-sacrificial love for others, you'll feel good, or people will like you. (But teachers are not honest enough to say it that simply; it sounds more "religious" to speak of "the search for inner peace" or "a sense of human community.")

THE FREEDOM OF DEATH

Both egresses—from the womb and from the world—are unfree, unwilling, unasked for. The two most important things that happen to us in this world are the only two in which we have absolutely no choice. How fortunate! For if we were asked, we would surely prefer the security of the womb, both wombs.

But if death is like birth, then "we're like eggs at present. And you can't just go on being a good egg forever. You must hatch or go bad."[21] The "immortality pill" would prevent us from hatching, and thus make us go bad. What a basket of rotten eggs a world of immortals would be! A deathless life would be like a birthless fetus or a hatchless egg. It would remove death's quarantine, death's tourniquet, death's barrier to the infinite expansion of our spiritual diseases. Our traditional wisdoms abound with myths of deathlessness as a curse: the Flying Dutchman, the Wandering Jew, Tithonus the Greek. Eternal life without God is not heaven; it is precisely hell. What a terrible thing death spares us from, from a fate worse than death. The seraphim's flaming sword barring the return to Eden is not only a punishment but also a mercy. Death is "a severe mercy":

> It is a safety-device because, once Man has fallen, natural immortality would be the one utterly hopeless destiny for him. Aided to the surrender that he must make [to God] by no external necessity of Death, free (if you call it freedom) to rivet faster and faster about himself through unending centuries the chains of his own pride and lust and of the nightmare civilizations which these build up in ever-increasing power and complication, he would progress from being merely a fallen man to being a fiend, possibly beyond all modes of redemption.[22]

But *is* death unfree? It *seems* unfree and passive—from this side of the door. So does birth, from this side of the womb. But if our analogy holds, then death, like birth, leads to greater freedom once the umbilical cord of dependence on Mother Earth is cut. After the involuntary plunge through the birth canal, voluntariness grows. "A man thrown into this world is like a plane catapulted into the air: he is launched by an external force, but then he must fly under his own power."[23]

We do not see this new freedom; but we do see the end of the old unfreedom. Death removes everything in us that is unfree, passive, and accidental, everything that we receive from this world through the umbilical cord of our body: our heredity, our environment, our possessions, our social status, our wealth. What remains is what is free, what we have freely made ourselves into, out of this worldly raw material, the person we have freely chosen to become. The clothes the world gave us now rot away; we stand as naked *I*'s in death: "Naked I came into this world; naked I return."[24]

In the Latin rite for the burial of an Austrian emperor, the people carry the corpse to the door of the great monastic church. The door is locked. They strike the door and say "Open!" The abbot inside says, "Who is there?" "Emperor Karl, King of X and Y and Z." "We know no such person here." Strike again. "Who is there?" "Emperor Karl." "We know no such person here." Strike a third time. "Who is there?" "Karl." The door is opened.

You can't take it with you—any "it." You can only take *you*.

AN ARGUMENT FOR IMMORTALITY

The distinction between the free, naked *I* and everything else puts us in a position to see why we must be immortal. A person not only *is* a body but *has* a body; that is, the "haver" is more than the "had." This "more" that every person is, is usually called the soul, or the spirit. What's that? Perhaps the best answer is that it is not a *what* at all; unlike everything else in the world, a person is not a *what* but a *who*, not an object but a subject. *What* I am is all my worldly clothes; *who* I am is their wearer, the naked self underneath. My heredity and environment have determined my *what* (for example, my race, sex, temperament, and taste for olives), but my free choices have determined my *who*. I am my own co-creator. Of course, my *what* has conditioned my *who;* that is, it has influenced it, both to limit it and to help it. But influencing is not forcing; conditioning is not determining. The world, which has given me my *what* by this determining, can and does take it all away in death. But since it has not given me my *who*, it cannot take it away, not even by death. If I am a person, I am immortal; if I am not immortal, I am not a person. *What* I am is not stronger than death, but *I* am. If I am not stronger than death, then I am not an I.

Another way of seeing this is that my anything and everything can die because it is possessed; it is what I *have*. There is a gap between me and what I have. The gap can become final, can become death. But I do not *have* my I; I *am* my I. There is no gap between I and I, as there is between me and mine; there is no place for death to fit, no "death-spot."[25] Death can separate me from everything, but not from myself.

Still another way is that a *what* is made of parts; therefore it is dissolvable into its parts; therefore, it can die. Not so with a *who*. Death is separation. Separation presupposes separable parts. The body dies because it is made of separable parts. Man dies because he is made of separable parts; that is, body and soul. But my soul, my *who,* my *I,* does not fall apart and die because it is one: it is me.

To say that death is not the end of me is not to say that death is irrelevant to me. It is my most radical transformation. It is my birth.

THE ECOLOGY OF DEATH

In birth there is (1) a new world—the earth, not the womb; (2) a new self—the baby, not the fetus; and (3) therefore, a new relation between self and world, between new organism and new environment—breathing, not the umbilical cord. The organism and the environment are ecologically related. If our thought experiment holds, death brings on something like these three ecologically related changes: (1) a new world, (2) a new self, and (3) therefore, a new relation between self and world.

1. There is a new world. The idea that the dead are ghosts (changed selves, bodiless spirits) haunting this same old world, would violate this point. So would the idea of reincarnation. Such ideas are a failure of the imagination. The only world they can imagine is the old world. They violate the basic law of ecology, that organism and environment are internally related. A new self cannot return to the old world any more than I can return to my mother's womb. That's why Jesus says to Nicodemus, "You must be born anew"; and when Nicodemus asks, "How can I be born when I am old? Can I enter a second time into my mother's womb?" Jesus replies, "What is born of flesh is flesh; what is born of Spirit is spirit."[26]

2. Anthropomorphic pictures of heaven, with us as we now are meeting our friends as they were, on the other side of the river of death is another, better land; or sitting on spiritual clouds playing mystical harps—such pictures violate the second of our three points. If there is a new world, there must be a new self too; if there is a transformed environment, there must be a transformed organism. Fish could not live outside water or fetuses outside wombs without learning to breathe. We could not live in heaven by breathing earthly air with earthly lungs. Its light could not be seen or endured by earthly eyes. We need new lungs, new eyes, a new body, "a spiritual body."[27] Dying is not only a change in the environment, like walking through a narrow door from a small, dark room into a larger, lighter one. It is a more radical

change than that. *Radical* means "concerning roots." Death uproots us completely from earthly soil and reroots us in new—not just new soil, but a new kind of soil. We therefore have to become new plants, not just go to new pots. Remember, death is not an ordinary door, a door between two parts of the same world, but a magic door, like a birth canal, from one world into another. Magic doors change whatever goes through them.

3. The new self after death is newly related to the new environment. The freer self is related more freely to the freer environment. The freer *environment* is a larger environment, with a greater range of choices, just as this world is a larger environment than the womb. The freer *self* is one with more ability to choose, both quantitatively and qualitatively, as the child is more able to choose than the fetus. And the *relation* between self and environment is freer, as walking and breathing is freer than the circulation of mother's blood in the womb. When a baby is outside the womb, he is freer and more independent, yet also more related to the whole of the world, than when he is inside.

WOMBS WITHIN WOMBS

A further consequence of our thought experiment is that just as the little world of the womb is part of the unimaginably larger world that opens up to us at birth, so this world is part of—and not apart from—an unimaginably larger world that opens up to us at death. Death is not entering a coffin, a confined box in the earth. It is precisely *leaving* a confined box in the earth! For that is what our present body is, a confined box in the earth.

The body, earth, mother, and matter—these four concepts have a primordial indentity. The "Earth Mother" is the basic myth. "Mother" and "Matter" come from the same linguistic roots. Both our mother and our earth are our greater body; narrowing the boundaries of the body to the epidermis is not innate but learned. I like to call it "epidermiolatry," idolatry of the epidermis.

The whole material universe is a maternal universe, a Great Mother, a womb. Its basic law, from galaxies to guppies, is growth, evolution, purposive change. Like a womb, it is not for itself or its own survival. It eventually grows old and dies. Its purpose is to mother a child. The human body is that child. The body is a womb within a womb, whose purpose it is in turn to mother the soul. Our body is a universe in miniature, a microcosm. It is also evolutionary, purposive, teleological, a growing instrument for a greater purpose, a place where something greater than itself is born, a birth canal within the cosmic birth canal, a door within a door.

And this womb within the universal womb, this body of ours, is larger on the inside than on the outside. Inner space is larger than outer space. Spirit is greater than matter. I am more than my body. In the Christian story, there was once a virgin's womb that was also larger on the inside than on the outside. What it contained, contained the whole world. Whether the story is historically true or not, it is a profound symbol of Everyman. Every human body is like Mary's body; it contains something bigger than the whole world. The world swallows our bodies like specks of dust; but our thought swallows the world.

> It is not in space that I must seek my human dignity, but in the ordering of my thoughts. It will do me no good to own land. Through space the universe grasps me and swallows me up like a speck; through thought I grasp it.[29]

The universe is a soul-making machine. Its gases and galaxies, its molecules and microorganisms, are nothing but its gears and wheels. They are not its point, its purpose. It exists not to produce suns but to produce sons, souls. The universe is our mother. Time is her pregnancy. "The whole creation has been groaning in travail together."[30] Our physical birth is her conception, the first appearance in time of this individual soul-baby. Our body's individual life is the universe's second pregnancy, a pregnancy within a pregnancy. Her first pregnancy bore our body; the second bears our soul. The goal of the first is a bodily life that ends in death, a life that gives itself up, like the placenta, to bear another life, a soul-baby. Life is a process down the cosmic birth canal, a "being-towards-death." The goal of the second pregnancy, the goal of our body's life, is also a death, a death to the womb-within-a-womb that is our body, for the purpose of being born into a deathless life. Our death is a mother. It gives itself up to bear life. As our life is a "being-towards-death," so our death is a "being-towards-life."

When we die, we move down the universe's birth canal, out of the cosmic mother, never to return to her womb. But perhaps not "never to return" to *her*. We may hope that when we have grown up in the larger world outside her, we can turn to her in new appreciation and love and understanding, just as an older child can do to his human mother. Once we are beyond her, we can be with her more truly:

> ... Come out, look back, and then you will see ... this astonishing cataract of bears, babies, and bananas: this immoderate deluge of atoms, orchids, oranges, cancers, canaries, fleas, gases, tornadoes and toads. ... Offer her neither worship nor contempt. Meet her and know her. If we are immortal, and if she is doomed (as the scientists tell us) to run down and die, we shall miss this half-shy and half-flamboyant creature, this ogress, this hoyden, this incorrigible fairy, this dumb witch. But the theologians tell us that she, like ourselves, is to be redeemed. The "vanity" to which she was subjected was her disease, not her essence. She will be cured, but cured in character: not tamed (Heaven forbid) nor sterilized. We shall still be able to recognize our old enemy, friend, playfellow and foster-mother, so perfected as to be not less, but more, herself. And that will be a merry meeting.[31]

DEATH IS NOT SEPARATION

Death seems to be a separation, an absenting, a ripping away of the organism from its environment. That is why death seems terrible, why it appears as an enemy. Nearly every example of joy or happiness or even pleasure seems to be an example of presence, of union—with a physical object, a person, God, beauty, or truth; and nearly every example of grief or sorrow seems to be an example of separation, of absence.

Death becomes acceptable *as part of presence* if we see it as our thought experiment does, as analogous to birth. When the umbilical cord is cut, the baby seems to be alone, alienated, lost to his mother. Yet he is not; he is less alone in the world than in the womb. He becomes capable for the first time of presence, of real union, of love, of I-Thou relationship.

This union, the union of comm-union, is not only happier and better but also more intimate, more unified, than the union of part to whole which exists in the womb. Love is the deepest kind of union. A finger cannot love a hand; a fetus cannot love its mother; there is no sound to one hand clapping. A child is more trúly one with its mother at thirty years than at three years, and more at three years than three months after conception. The deepest meaning of the word *one* is not quantitative but qualitative, not mathematical but maternal.

The farther away from its mother the child grows, in independence and individuality, the deeper the possibility of union through mature love. For the individual ego exists for this purpose: to be given away in love, thus to be truly found:

> This is the ultimate law—the seed dies to live, the bread must be cast upon the waters, he that loses his soul will save it. . . . For union exists only between distincts; and perhaps, from this point of view, we catch a momentary glimpse of the meaning of all things. Pantheism is a creed not so much false as hopelessly behind the times. Once, before creation, it would have been true to say that everything was God. But God created: He caused things to be other than Himself that, being distinct, they might learn to love Him, and achieve union instead of mere sameness. Thus he also cast His bread upon the waters. . . . Even within the Holy One Himself, it is not sufficient that the Word should *be* God, it must also be *with* God. The Father eternally begets the Son and the Holy Ghost proceeds: deity introduces distinction within itself so that the union of reciprocal loves may transcend mere arithmetical unity or self identity. . . .
>
> For in self-giving, if anywhere, we touch a rhythm not only of all creation but of all being. For the Eternal Word also gives Himself in sacrifice; and that not only on Calvary. For when He was crucified, He "did that in the wild weather of His outlying provinces which He had done at home in glory and gladness." [32] From before the foundation of the world He surrenders begotten Deity back to begetting Deity in obedience. . . . From the highest to the lowest, self exists to be abdicated and, by that abdication, becomes the more truly self, to be thereupon yet the more abdicated, and so forever. This is not a heavenly law which we can escape by remaining earthly, nor an earthly law which we can escape by being saved. What is outside the system of self-giving is not earth, nor nature, nor "ordinary life," but simply and solely Hell. [33]

Love performs the contradictory, impossible feat of uniting by individuating and individuating by uniting. "At what moment do two lovers come into the most complete possession of themselves if not when they say that they are lost in each other." [34]

Through the death of the old dependence on mother, new independence and individuality emerge. These in turn are raw material for new relationships, new unions. A relationship of love is neither one of dependence nor one of mere independence. The opposition between these opposing categories is transcended when the categories themselves are transcended. A lover is neither a part of (and thus dependent on) nor apart from (and thus independent of) his beloved, but *with* her.

The category of with-ness (*co-esse*) is one of the most important and neglected categories in philosophy.[35]

The absence of a lover, caused by death, does not sever this *co-esse*. Love is stronger than death. It seems at first that death is mere absence, as it would seem to the baby being born that birth is absence and separation. Later it appears as another, deeper mode of presence. These two apperances are lived through in C. S. Lewis's *A Grief Observed:* first the apparent absence, then the real presence:

> We both knew this. I had my miseries, not hers; she had hers, not mine. . . . We were setting out on different roads. This cold truth, this terrible traffic-regulation ("You, Madam, to the right—you, Sir to the left") is just the beginning of the separation which is death itself. . . . she used to quote, "Alone into the Alone." She said it felt like that. And how immensely improbable that it should be otherwise! Time and space and body were the very things that brought us together; the telephone wires by which we communicated. Cut one off, or cut both off simultaneously. Either way, mustn't the conversation stop?

No!—

> And then one or other dies. And we think of this as love cut short; like a dance stopped in mid-career or a flower with its head unluckily snapped off . . . [But] bereavement is a universal and integral part of our experience of love. It follows marriage as normally as marriage follows courtship or as winter follows autumn. It is not a truncation of the process but one of its phases; not the interruption of the dance, but the next figure. We are "taken out of ourselves" by the loved one while she is here. Then comes the tragic figure of the dance in which we most learn to be still taken out of ourselves though the bodily presence is withdrawn, to love the very Her, and not fall back to loving our past, or our memory, or our sorrow, or our relief from sorrow, or our own love.[36]

The "tragic figure of the dance" produces an even closer presence than the earthly marriage could have done. For a person is "bigger on the inside than on the outside," and death brings a person closer by removing the outside once it has done its work. Death unsheathes the sword; death strips us for the naked embrace.

UNION WITH THE WORLD THROUGH DEATH

Death not only unites us more closely with our beloved; it also unites us more closely with the whole world, as a mother unites her baby more closely with the whole world by giving birth. Our present body is both fatal and fetal. Like a fetus, it is extremely limited; it can unite us only with that portion of the whole that is somehow received or derived from our five senses. The body into which we are born at death transcends these fetal limitations. Such a body is invisible to us now, of course. This should not surprise us if we think in terms of our thought experiment paralleling death and birth: the present body is just as invisible to a fetus.

One way death unites us with the whole world is through a marvelous kind of time-transcending remembering. At the moment of death, according to widespread testimony,[37] we remember and review the whole of our life in detail at a single moment. This seems to be more-than-time remembering time, as some archetypal dreams may be time remembering less-than-time. Such dreams seem to be our remembering of our womb consciousness; they are the navel of our psyche, our souvenir from our travels on the former side of the magic door of birth.

Death also unites us with the whole world in a deeper way than merely remembering the whole of our life, if it is a mother. A fetus's body relates it only to a tiny part of the world we know (though it is all of the world the fetus knows): its mother's womb. The born person's body relates him to the whole world we now know. But this world in turn is only a tiny part of a much larger world.[38] The after-death body relates the after-death person to the whole of that world. But this world is included in that world, as a womb is included in this world. As a born person understands the meaning of a womb better than a fetus, a dead person understands the meaning of this world better than a living one, as Emily does in *Our Town*.

Oriental mysticism is an attempt to unite with and to understand the meaning of the whole of the world before experiencing death. This is why it is a flight from the body and the ego that identifies itself with its body, the body that limits us to *this* and not *all*. There are three philosophies of man's essence: Western secularism says man is simply finitude and matter; Eastern mysticism says man is simply infinity and spirit; Christianity (and Judaism and Islam) says man is both matter and finite spirit in relation to infinity. The first says this body is everything we are; the second says this body is nothing we truly are; the third says this body is the seed, or fetus, of what we truly are.

Christianity is a sacramental religion ultimately because Jesus attained an intimate union with the world, with matter, not just by his incarnation but by his death. He went down to the roots of the cosmic tree and reinvigorated its sap. The image imposes itself of a gigantic Atlas humbly stooping lower than the lowest in order to bear the burden of the whole of reality on his shoulders, then straightening up and bursting through the primordial darkness into the heavenly sunlight. It is *this* death that a Christian dies "in Christ."

WHY WE MUST DIE

Death as a mother answers Zorba the Greek's question "Why must anybody die? Tell me." I must die to be born. The body must die because it has served its purpose and is worn out, like the placenta. It is as though nature cannot wait to reclaim what was hers, that body that would have obeyed only nature's laws of physics and chemistry if it were subject only to them, but that was used as the instrument of the spirit for a while. As soon as the spirit departs, the body begins to disintegrate, just as when the hand wielding the sword lets go, the sword drops, obeying the laws of gravity rather than the will of the wielder.

It is good that the body gets worn out. It is even good that it ages before it dies, for that makes it easier for us to abandon it. We naturally cling to it; bodily self-preservation is our most deeply rooted instinct, Mother Nature's first commandment. Aging teaches us a higher law; we learn detachment from the old womb when the time for birth approaches.

Reincarnation would be intolerable, like repeating kindergarten, or having triplets at age fifty, or hearing the same symphony twelve times in a row. Enough is enough. We need not to repeat the dream of life but to wake up. "One short sleep past, we wake eternally."[39]

This explains why infants sleep most, old people least. Infants sleep most because they have been sleeping since the foundation of the world, and the habit is not easily broken. (Of course there are physiological reasons too; but they do not exclude other, higher reasons.) This life is also a sleep, though not so deep a one. We are weaned from the habit gradually. It is appropriate that old people sleep less than young, for they are closer to eternal wakefulness, closer to the divesting of the habit of sleep altogether.

Those who catch a glimpse of the next life, whether by mysticism, divine revelation, or resuscitation, always use images of waking, not of sleep. They never speak of eternal rest. Buddha calls himself "the man who woke up." Mystical experience is called "enlightenment." Resuscitated patients report seeing a "being of light."[40] The Book of Revelation says of heaven, "There is no night there."[41] In the womb there is no day; in the world there is both day and night; in heaven there is no night.

DEATH WEANS US FROM DEATH

But do we desire the day? Do we want to wake up? Freud detects in us two fundamental drives or desires.[42] *Eros,* the life instinct, and *thanatos,* the death instinct, lead us in opposite directions in pursuit of happiness. *Eros* is the creative drive, the forward push. For Freud, it is primarily sexual, even genital; but all forms of creativity, including art and science, are erotic. *Thanatos* is the desire to return to a womblike state where no desire is frustrated, where desire does not exceed gratification. In the light of these categories, the function of death as a mother is to wean us. From what? From *thanatos*—that is, from death—from comfort, security, sleeping, dreaming—from the womb. Modern man especially needs death because he is history's greatest comfort and security monger, and, as we saw in Chapter 2, the deepest meaning of technology is as a tool to that end. Our society's comfort-dispensing machines are turning the world into a huge womb, where nearly every desire can be instantly gratified. And ironically, that so-ciety which above all needs death is on the verge of inventing the "immortality pill" to avoid it. This is technology's supreme triumph.

Death delivers us from a terrible thing, a fate worse than death. This terrible thing is something which our American Constitution calls one of our three fundamental rights! Not life, not liberty, but the pursuit of happiness is a terrible thing. In fact, one must choose either life (*eros*) and liberty *or* the pursuit of happiness, if we mean happiness in the modern, rather than the ancient, sense. The modern sense of happiness is subjective contentment, not objective perfection, not the fulfillment of the ontological purpose for which we exist. For us, if you think you're happy, you're happy. The ancients (such as Solomon, Plato, Aristotle, Augustine, Aquinas) would disagree: A fool thinks he is happy, but he is a fool.

Now this pursuit of happiness in the modern sense is really the death-wish, *thanatos*. Therefore, it is contrary to real liberty. Therefore modern man reinterprets liberty as he reinterprets happiness. Liberty is no longer freedom *to* attain my true, objective end, but freedom *from* obstacles and frustrations to my subjective desires; it is not freedom *from* a womb but the freedom *of* a womb.

It is a fate worse than physical death, for physical death kills only the body, while *thanatos* kills the spirit and its life, its drive, its *eros*. I have taught classes of students who thought *Brave New World* a utopia rather than a dystopia, and envied it; who were so stuck into the "do your own thing" philosophy that they said they would not "impose their values" on others by preventing a loved one from committing suicide or a son or daughter from spending his whole life playing with mud pies "if it made him happy." We moderns show in thousands of ways that our ideals are rarely higher than elaborate mud pies, that we would rather live in comfortable dreams than confront reality. Do we even believe that the word *reality* has any clear meaning, that the distinction between the real and the unreal is objectively identifiable? Subjectivism and relativism is a comfortably womblike philosophy.

We are *thanatos* addicts, and death frees us from this addiction. Death is not thanatopic; death is erotic. It is like birth—it plunges us into the unavoidable light of objective reality.

We hate that light. This is why we kill most of our prophets and wise men, from Socrates and Jesus to Gandhi and Martin Luther King: because they tell the truth. They are lights, and mirrors, and alarm clocks; more, they are midwives. We would rather hide or sink into the womb. We need death as we need birth. It forces us, against our will, to grow, just as suffering forces our minds, against our will, to grow to wisdom:

> Hour by hour, drop by drop
> Pain falls upon the heart
> And against our will
> And even in our own despair
> Comes wisdom from the awful grace of God.[43]

From Socrates and Solomon to Kierkegaard and Nietzsche, philosophers contrast the pursuit of pleasure with the pursuit of wisdom. Truth is a severe master, not a gentle one. We prefer tolerance to truth, kindness to love, compassion to idealism. We relate better to grandfathers than fathers. If the real Socrates, the real Jesus, or the real Buddha, as distinct from the harmless pastel figures of the selective modern imagination, were alive today, they would be hated as being too hard, too demanding, too "inhuman."

Progress in human history, according to Toynbee, is largely a matter of "challenge and response."[44] Man moved ahead only where he was kicked in the pants. Death is the ultimate kick in the pants.

The "immortality pill" is our kick back. It is the apotheosis of modern man's new *summum bonum,* the conquest of nature. Death is the last natural power to be conquered. The Pill will be the fulfillment of one of our deepest and darkest dreams, the Oedipus complex. Now we will be able to kill our father (God), and marry our mother (earth). For without death, and with an earthly technological paradise, we no longer want God or Heaven. We can now return with our phallic power of technology into our birth canal; we can impregnate Mother Earth with our life forever. It is the supreme obscenity of man's history, and the supreme illustration of the greatest of paradoxes, that "he that findeth his life shall lose it; and he that loseth his life shall find it."[45]

DEATH AS AN OPERATION

But man need not have this incestuous relationship with earth. Incest is the perversion of the mother-child relationship, not its essence. Possessiveness (on the part of the mother) is also a perversion of the mother-child relationship, not its essence. Death is not a possessive mother. Death means for us to grow.

The growth is spiritual, and moral. Death is our moral mother, our supreme instrument for moral growth. When Jesus says, "Blessed are those who hunger and thirst after righteousness, for they shall be filled,"[46] he is talking about death. If we seek righteousness, we will not fear death but look forward to it, for in death we finally attain our goal. In death we finally become unable to sin, "dead to sin."[47] Death is the supreme healing operation. All of life is "pre-op."

How does this work? By a kind of anaesthesia. Only in death are we able to stop fighting the divine surgeon, able to stop saying "*my* will be done" instead of "Thy will be done." Only in death can the very roots of our being, where sin is, be conquered and healed. Only in death can we be radically remade from within:

> We can set no limits to the tearing up of roots that is involved in our journey into God. . . . There is a further step to take: the one that makes us lose all foothold within ourselves. . . . What will be the agent of that definitive transformation? Nothing less than death. . . . The great victory of the Creator and Redeemer, in the Christian vision, is to have transformed what is in itself a universal power of diminishment and extinction into an essentially life-giving factor. God must, in some way or other, make room for himself, hollowing us out and emptying us, if he is finally to penetrate into us. And in order to assimilate us in him, he must break the molecules of our being so as to re-cast and remodel us. The function of death is to provide the necessary entrance into our inmost selves.[48]

Why is such radical surgery necessary? Not only becuase of the radical disease (sin, separation from God) but also because we must be made totally receptive in order to be united with God because God cannot be the possessed, only the Possessor. God impregnates us, we do not impregnate Him. This is why He is imaged as a "He," not a "She": the sexual symbolism is appropriate to the spiritual relationship. God's essence is I AM—the subject, not the object, the living and active one, the First. Nothing can ever be what it essentially is not. Therefore God can never be an object. Therefore He can never be an object of human having, only the Haver.

Now our body is the foundation for all our having, the instrument by which we possess. The spirit or self cannot have, possess, grasp, or hoard:

> The heart of man cannot hoard. His brain or his hand may gather into its box and hoard, but the moment things have passed into the box, the heart has lost them and is hungry again.[49]

Death removes the body, therefore removes having—so that God can then unite Himself with us in the only way possible, as Haver, not had, as Subject, not object, as I AM—that is, as He really is.

This union is the great marriage, the point of all life and history and creation, the supreme consummation of all existence. We need another chapter to explore this final face of death, the face to which we have been led by death's motherhood: the face of death as our lover.

NOTES

1. See Mircea Eliade, *The Sacred and the Profane* (New York: Harcourt, Brace, 1959).
2. Erik Erikson, Freud's maverick disciple, noted that infants who had not been conditioned by their environment to any sexist roles or stereotypes nevertheless persisted in spontaneously playing with blocks in sexually differentiated ways; the vast majority of infant girls made concave (womb-like) shapes and the vast majority of infant boys made convex (phallic) shapes. See *Childhood and Society* (New York: W. W. Norton, 1950).
3. The word is *sēmeion;* see, for example, John 2:11.
4. For example, Rev. 19:13.
5. John 10:7, 9.
6. See *The New Catholic Dictionary* (New York: Universal Knowledge Foundation, 1929), p. 844; *The New Catholic Encyclopedia* (New York: McGraw-Hill, 1967), vol. 5 ("ex opere operato") and vol. 12 ("sacraments").
7. Ibid.; *The New Catholic Dictionary* defines a sacrament as both "significative and productive of grace," p. 844.
8. Matt. 27:50–51.
9. Matt. 27:52–53.
10. Judg. 14:14.
11. Matt. 27:46.
12. It is also the wisdom of the cartoonist! Johnny Hart, in his "B.C.," has a baby dinosaur hatching out of his egg look around and exclaim: "It's true; there *is* life after birth!"
13. Thomas Howard, *Splendor in the Ordinary* (Wheaton, Ill.: Tyndale House, 1977), pp. 23–24.
14. John 14:27.
15. Augustine *Confessions* 1. 1.
16. Charles Kingsley, *Health and Education: The Science of Health,* 1874. The text reads: "To be discontented with the divine discontent, and to be ashamed with the noble shame, is the very germ and first upgrowth of all virtue."
17. Eccles. 3:11
18. Eccles. 2:19.
19. See Raymond Moody, *Life After Life* (New York: Bantam Books, 1976), p. 25ff.
20. Ibid., p. 73ff.
21. C. S. Lewis, *Mere Christianity* (New York: Macmillan, 1960).
22. C. S. Lewis, *Miracles* (New York: Macmillan, 1955), p. 156.
23. Roger Troisfontaines, "The Mystery of Death," in *The Mystery of Suffering and Death,* ed. Michael J. Taylor, S.J. (New York: Doubleday Image Books, 1974), p. 185.
24. Job 1:21.
25. See Lao Tzu *Tao Te Ching* 50.
26. John 3:3.
27. 1 Cor. 15, esp. vs. 44.
28. See Augustine *Sermon* 15 (Christmas).
29. Pascal, *Prensées,* 113. (trans. Krailsheimer). above, p. 59.
30. Rom. 8:22.
31. Lewis, *Miracles,* pp. 80–81.
32. George MacDonald, *Unspoken Sermons,* Third Series (London; New York: George Rutledge & Sons, 1873), pp. 11–12.

33. C. S. Lewis, *The Problem of Pain* (New York: Macmillan, 1962), pp. 149–152.
34. Pierre Teilhard de Chardin, *The Phenomenon of Man,* trans. Bernard Wall (New York: Harper & Row, 1959), p. 265.
35. See Gabriel Marcel, *Being and Having,* trans. Katherine Farrer (Boston: Beacon Press, 1951), pp. 137, 237; *The Mystery of Being,* vol. 1, trans. G.S. Fraser (Chicago: Regnery, 1951), p. 77; vol. 2, trans. René Hague (Chicago: Regnery, 1951), p. 9; *Metaphysical Journal,* trans. Bernard Wall (Chicago: Regnery, 1952), p. 170; *Du refus à l'invocation* (Paris: Librairie Gallimard, 1940), pp. 50–52.
36. C. S. Lewis, *A Grief Observed* (New York: Seabury Press, 1963), pp. 14–15, 58–59, 63–64.
37. See Raymond Moody, *Life After Life* (New York: Bantam Books, 1976), pp. 64ff.
38. See William James on this in *Varieties of Religious Experience.* (London, N.Y.: Longmans, Green, 1909; New Hyde Park, N.Y.: University Books, 1963.)
39. John Donne, "Death, Be Not Proud,"
40. Moody, *Life After Life,* pp. 58ff.
41. Rev. 21:15, 22:5.
42. See *Civilization and its Discontents; Beyond the Pleasure Principle;* and *The Ego and the Id.*
43. Aeschylus, "Agamemnon"; cf. Richard Lattimore's translation in *Aeschylus I* in *The Complete Greek Tragedies* (New York: Washington Square Press, 1967), p. 44.
44. See Arnold Toynbee, *A Study of History* (New York and London: Oxford University Press, 1947).
45. Matt. 10:39.
46. Matt. 5:6.
47. Rom. 6, esp. vss. 2, 11.
48. Pierre Teilhard de Chardin, *The Divine Milieu* (New York: Harper & Row, 1960), pp. 88–89.
49. George MacDonald, quoted in C. S. Lewis, *George MacDonald: An Anthology,* no. 287, p. 119 (New York: Macmillan, 1978).

CHAPTER 5

Death as a Lover

A STRANGE EXPERIENCE

I had a very strange experience while writing this book. Its basic image is death personified; we look at death as if it were a person wearing five masks or five faces. "Personification" means treating what is not a person as if it were a person. But as I entered more deeply into my exploration of death, it seemed more and more to *be* a person. (Who, I wondered?—and therein lies the final secret.) However strongly my rational mind told me that this was mere personification, mere imagination, mere projection of a subjective fiction, something else told me otherwise. This "something else" *bumped up against* the real personality of death as an objective discovery, not a subjective creation; a meeting, not a making; a person, not a personification.

More and more I came to look forward to this meeting, to returning to this book where I met death, cherished its presence, explored its fascinating country. It was not merely the attractive task of writing, but the prospect of fulfilling a promise—as if death and I had covenanted a rendezvous, as if we belonged to each other, as if we were lovers—as if death were my bride. I thought of Shakespeare's line: "I will encounter darkness as a bride and hug it in mine arms."[1]

But that image doesn't really fit the experience. It was more as if I were death's bride. To be a new bride must be a strange and stirring experience; even a male can share a little of its wonder by empathy and imagination, through his own *anima*, his spirit's female side. Before the age of sexual "liberation" and the removal of mystery and magic and wonder from sex, a bride often felt a strange mixture of anticipation and apprehension on her wedding night. She both trusted and trembled before her lover, like the earth before the awesome hour of the dawn. This is exactly how I felt about my lover death. I felt a strangely exhilarating confusion: I could not tame death, but I had to do something with him (the "it" had now become a "him"!); I couldn't get along *with* him (for he is an enemy) and I couldn't get along *without* him (for he is a friend), so I had to either ignore him (as a stranger) or marry him (as a lover).

Death as mother did not fit this experience. Death as a mother is not sufficient; we must explore further. For death is not natural, like a mother. There is nothing more natural than a mother ("Mother Nature"), and nothing more unnatural than death. Birth is natural, but death is not merely like birth. It is not merely a part of the great, natural cosmic process that inevitably leads to growth and greater life. It is that, but it is also not that. In at least three ways it is not like that: it is individual; it is free, active choice; and it is meeting—like love. We must explore each of these three features of the face of death as a lover.

THE INDIVIDUALITY OF DEATH

Love is individual:

> I adjure you, O daughters of Jerusalem,
>   if you find my beloved,
> That you tell him
>   I am sick with love.
>
> What is your beloved more than another beloved,
>   O fairest among women?
> What is your beloved more than another beloved,
>   that you thus adjure us?
>
> My beloved is all radiant and ruddy,
>   distinguished among ten thousand.
> His head is the finest gold . . . .
>
> There are sixty queens and eighty concubines,
>   and maidens without number.
> My dove, my perfect one, is only one.[2]

Death can be a lover because death, like love, is individual. The truest face of death is not cosmic; death means *my* death, not death in general. I die as an individual because I live as an individual.

I exist also as part of a whole, an ingredient in the cosmic recipe; but I am not merely that. I am that as an object, a thing, a knowable, classifiable, placeable and therefore replaceable thing. But in my deeper reality as a person, as a subject, as an *I,* I am a unique center of the cosmos, not a replaceable ingredient in it. As conscious and reflective, I am like a mirror, reflecting the whole cosmos in my consciousness. A mirror, like a person, is both object and subject. As an object, a body, a thing, it is merely a silvered piece of glass, so large, in such a place and no other. But as a mirror, it is a reflection of the whole world. Like human consciousness, it gives a second life to all objects that appear in it.

I too am a mirror of the whole world, not just an opaque thing in the world. As a mirror, I am an image of God; my *I* is an image of the absolute I. As my mirror mirrors the world, God's mirror mirrors me and all other persons. I am the world's God and God's world, the world's subject and God's object, the world's I and God's *Thou.* I give the world a second, higher life in human consciousness by reflecting it in my mirror, and God gives me a higher life, a divine and eternal life, by reflecting me in His mirror.

MY DIVINE NAME

"I" is my divine name. Once and once only in Bible does God reveal His true name, and this is the name: I AM. Every other name of God is anthropomorphic, relative to man. Names like "God," "Lord," "Creator," and "Redeemer" tell what God is in relation to Man, not what God is in Himself. He never says "I am *My* God," only "I am *your* God." But to Moses[3] God tells His inmost secret, the name I AM, JHWH, the Sacred Tetragrammaton. No orthodox Jew ever pronounces this word. The reason is this: Only God can speak this name truly. He who speaks any other name than this one, either *expresses* (in the third person) or *addresses* (in the second person) the bearer of the name he speaks; but he who speaks this name *possesses* it (first person). For instance, if I say "Oscar," I do not claim to speak as Oscar, only to speak *to* Oscar or to speak *about* Oscar. I either address or express Oscar; I do not possess Oscar. I *am* not Oscar. But to say "I" is to possess I. To say "I AM" is to claim to *be* "I AM." Only I AM can speak the private name.

(This is why, when Jesus was asked "Who do you claim to be?" and answered "Truly, truly I say to you, Before Abraham was, I AM!"[4]— he uttered the ultimate blasphemy if he was only a man; and the Jews were quite right to try to stone him. Death by stoning was the penalty for blasphemy according to Old Testament law.)

Man is the image of God because he too is "I." *No one else can speak this name.* What a mysterious thing is this "I"—how utterly private! My "I" is not your "I" but your "you," and your "I" is not my "I" but my "you." I can share everything but this. I can share a world, but not my "I." I can share my thoughts, my feelings, my love—but not my "I." It is my unique core, essence, center, and reality. The thing Buddha calls the ultimate illusion and the cause of all suffering is for the Jew and the Christian the ultimate reality, real in me because real in God, real in me as image because real in God as original.

My death, like my self, is private and individual. Death is "in each case *mine*."[5] Seeing death as a mother does not yet do justice to this individuality. It tends toward pantheism, the great cosmic process, the womb of the world, emergent evolution, the necessary cycle of nature, and all that sort of thing. It is death that transcends all that sort of thing, not birth. I am not much of an individual at birth; in fact, I am just barely an individual at birth. "Born a man, died a grocer," says the cynical French epitaph; but it should be "Born a fetus, died an individual." (Kierkegaard wanted on his tombstone the simple epitaph "the individual.") There is only one me, but there are many grocers; so "died a grocer" means "died *not* an individual." Death is the invitation to individuality; we can accept or decline the invitation.

Death is the supreme invitation to individuality. For death is the one thing I must do all my myself. No one can do it for me. I am alone. In fact, the essence of death is aloneness, separation; and this is its tragedy. In death we are (it seems) severed from our body, from our world, from our friends, and even (it seems) from God. Even Jesus died this complete death, this total aloneness: "My God, my God, why hast Thou forsaken me?" If this is God dying man's death, then even God must die alone, because man dies alone.

Death culminates and consummates our loneliness. We are each born with a secret, a secret we try to hide every second of our lives by a million clever devices, both internal and external. The secret is that each of us is terribly alone, each finds that loneliness unendurable, each reaches out desperately to overcome it in those million ways, never fully succeeds, and cannot admit that failure. Our essence, our "I," is not shareable, no matter how hard we try. Death finally reveals this terrible fact.

What is the meaning of this loneliness? What is its purpose, its end, its finality? What is individuality *for?* In life, it is for union, for meeting, for relationships, for love. I am alienated so that I can overcome alienation. I become an individual self so that I may give myself to another and receive another's self. The paradox of *agapē*, of self-giving love, is that it does the impossible, the thing we have just said cannot be done. It shares the unshareable, gives the ungiveable, and receives from the other the gift that can no more be received than given: the gift of self, the gift of the giver, the *I*. *Agapē*, as distinct from *eros* (desire) or *philia* (friendship) or *storgē* (affection),[6] is a gift not just of pleasure, or the body, or possessions, or time, or actions, or interests, or feelings, or thoughts, but of self.

There is a second paradox to *agapē:* it performs the apparently contradictory feat of individuating by uniting, as well as uniting by individuating. The self, once given, is found. "He who loses his self shall find it."[7]

A third paradox is that the union of *agapē* is a closer union than the union of identity. I am more one with my beloved than I am with myself:

The final end of . . . separation . . . is not individuality; that is but a means to it. The final end is oneness—an impossibility without it. For there can be no unity, no delight of love, no harmony, no good in being, where there is but one. Two at least are needed for oneness. . . . For of no onehood comes unity; there can be no oneness where there is only one. For the very beginnings of unity there must be two. . . . For God made our individuality as well as, and a greater marvel than, our dependence; made our apartness from Himself, that freedom should bind us divinely nearer to Himself with a new and inscrutable marvel of love . . . the freer the man, the stronger the bond that binds him to Him who made his freedom.[8]

Individuality, then, is for love. No one can love who is not an individual; no one can overcome aloneness who is not first alone. Death enables us to be completely alone—in nothing else are we *completely* alone—and thus death enables us to be completely together. If we did not know death, we could not know love. Love and death, apparently enemies, are really in symbiosis. For in order to love, we must be individuals; to be individuals, we must know death; therefore, in order to love, we must know death.

More, love itself is a kind of death. That is, if I do not love, I see myself as the sun, and others as planets in my solar system, walk-ons in my play, ingredients in my recipe. I am what Sartre calls "being-for-itself" (subject), and others are reduced to "being-in-itself" (objects).[9] Love overcomes this dualism, this alienation, this split into two kinds of being. For love dies to solarity, to being the sun, to egotism; love means a living ego dying to egotism. The paradox of a nonegotistic ego comes about through the ego dying to itself and living in and through that death—an immortality of the dying ego. Buddha sees no such possibility, an ego without egotism; therefore, he teaches egolessness. Sartre sees no such possibility; he sees all men as egotists.[10] So does Freud, for different reasons.[11] There are essentially three philosophies of man,[12] three philosophies of life: Eastern mysticism, Western secularism, and Biblical theism. The first simply denies the ego as illusion, as dead; the second simply affirms its natural life; and the third sees it as something that truly lives only by dying.

FREE DEATH

Love is free. It does not rape; it seduces, it "draws":

O that you *would* kiss me with the kisses of your mouth!
For your love is better than wine. . . .

Draw me after you, let us make haste. . . .

I adjure you, O daughters of Jerusalem,
    by the gazelles or the hinds of the field,
that you stir not up nor awaken love
    until it please.[13]

Death can be a lover because death, like love, is free. This is a second reason why death's deepest face is not that of a mother: unlike being born, dying is a free act. Obviously, *whether* I die is not free, but *how* I die is. Birth is not free, for at birth I am not yet a fully conscious self. But death is free because at death I am a fully conscious self; in fact, *only* at death am I a *fully* conscious self. My life is complete and becomes for the first time a complete object of my consciousness; my whole life passes before me at death. Birth is my most supremely passive and unfree act; death is my most supremely active and free act; therefore death is more than birth.

How is death free? Only death presents us with an ultimately free choice because only death presents us with an ultimate choice. All other choices are, first of all, repentable, reversible, because we have some time left, we have a future. In the second place, every other choice is a choice of the final end through some means; the end is chosen not purely and absolutely but relatively, implicitly, in and through the means. In the third place, all other choices are made with a part of ourselves: that part that exists in this partial time, which is not all my time, and (in the fourth place) that part which has only partial knowledge of the end, the good, the goal. These four conditions are overcome in death. There is no more future, so that the last choice is irreversible; there are no more means, so the last choice is a choice of the absolute end absolutely; there is no more spilling out of the self along the shallow floor of time, so the last choice is made with the whole, completed self; and there is now full knowledge, and no evasion of the light. This is total freedom for the first time in my life—in my death.

CHOOSING LIFE

The ultimate free choice is "a matter of life and death." "I call heaven and earth to witness against you this day, that I have set before you life and death, blessing and curse; therefore choose life."[14] But don't we always choose life? No. Moses' speech to Israel implies that all evil is choosing death. Free choice is choice between good and evil, and this is a choice between life and death—the life and death of the soul, the spirit, the I, the choosing self. Goodness is the life of the soul; evil is its death. The essential moral imperative is: Choose life.

But how can death be called a lover if we are to choose life? Are we not to choose our lover?

Of course we are to choose our lover. And of course we are to choose life. But death is still our lover because death is life's mask. Behind the mask of death as a lover, the last face of death, lies life. The one who wears the masks of death is life. But we can meet this life only through death. Strip off death's four other masks and you see death as a lover; strip off the last mask and you see not death but life. But in order for death to be our lover, we must *choose* the life that wears death's mask. Life comes to us masked as death, Beauty as the Beast. Death is the free opportunity to choose life.

That statement needs some explanation. Death does not seem like an opportunity; death does not seem like a choice; and death does not seem like life. How can one say that death is the free opportunity to choose life?

Death is the act of freely presenting to God my complete life and the completed self I have constructed by every free choice I have ever made. For my choices have created not just my behavior but my self, by a kind of rebound: the axe that weakens the tree also toughens the lumberjack, and the crime that weakens the victim also hardens the criminal. In shaping our world we are shaping our selves. God has given the human creature the incredible dignity of collaborating in its own creation, of being present at the moment of its own creation. God supplies only the raw material: existence (through creation), heredity (through evolution) and environment (through providence). These make me *what* I am, but *who* I am is up to me. The form I construct out of this matter, the statue I sculpt out of this marble, is mine and is me. Life is art, *poiēma,* making—in fact, self-making, self-creation. And the supreme act of self-creation is the act of dying.

No choice made before death is made by my completed self as the choosing subject, nor is it a choice *of* my completed self as chosen object, because while it lives in time, the self is not completed but still in process of completing itself, choice by choice. Until the last second there is always the remote but real possibility of undoing many choices, such as a deathbed repentance or betrayal. Death is the end of all temporal possibilities; death makes me eternally actual. It boils me down, distils me to my essence, rolls me into a ball, and throws me into the eternal game. Life is like a line; each choice is like the next point on that line; death is like the last point on the line, which is the whole line when looked at end-on, from ahead, from eternity. Death is the *point* of life. Death is my total and unchangeable response to the last and greatest question: Who are you?

Seeing death as the opportunity to choose life is seeing it as the opportunity to choose God. The nature of God is expressed especially by three words by St. John and many other Christian mystics: *life, light,* and *love* (strikingly similar to the Hindu *sat, chit,* and *ananda*). Death as my last act is my final choice for or against God as life, light, and love. It happens at the moment of death, not before. Now finally all the means are gone; I am face to face with my end. My choice is absolute, pure, simple, naked, and direct. If throughout my life I have created habits of character that make me life, light, and love-seeking, I will find it "second nature" to choose God. If I have created a self with loveless, lightless, and lifeless habits, it will be difficult (though, we may hope, still possible with much purgation and painful education).

The decision at death is the essence of all decisions: for or against all value. Light, life, and love parallel the three absolute values of truth, goodness, and beauty, the supreme values of the three parts of the soul; intellect, will, and emotions. God is all truth, goodness, and beauty; everything that is true, good, or beautiful is a reflection of God, a participation in God, a shadow of God. Therefore every choice for or against any truth, any goodness or any beauty is a choice for or against God—whether He is known or unknown, named or anonymous. A choice to change a diaper, praise a sunset, admit a mistake, or give up a subway seat is a choice for God: "Inasmuch as ye did it unto one of the least of these My brothers, ye did it unto Me." [15]

DEATH IS NOT PASSIVE

But death still does not *seem* to be a free, active choice. From this side of death's door, it seems passive and unfree. However, a door has two sides. If, following our thought experiment, there exists on the other side of death a world of spirit, then that world is a world of free activity (for it is matter that accounts for passivity). The door into the world of time, matter, and passivity is birth; it is a temporal, material, and passive door. The door into the world of eternity, spirit, and activity is death, which is not such a door, not a temporal, material, and passive change. From this side of the door, death looks like such a change; from the world of passivity, death looks passive. But from the other side of the door, death will be seen to be an act.

We see death as passive and unfree only because we objectify it, we reduce it to an event in nature. When we observe another person's death as an object, we see the passive, the negative, the departure. The tide seems to take the ship from the shore. But when *we* are the ship, we *take* the tide. When death is individual, death is active.

If death is passive, as it seems, then it contradicts the meaning of human life. For the meaning of life is love, and love is an act; the act of affirming the other freely. If death as the crowning event in life is passive, then life ends "not with a bang but a whimper,"[16] and it is ultimately a joke, a tease, a come-on, a promise not fulfilled. Worse: It is a dirty joke, a scandal, a cosmic obscenity.

MEETING

We have seen that death is more than a mother because it is individual and because it is a free act. The third reason death is more than a mother is that being born is not meeting, but death is meeting. Being born is the necessary condition for meeting, for communion and community and communication; but being born is not yet meeting. Death is. "There once lived a people who had a profound understanding of the divine; this people thought that no man could see God and live."[17] But "all real living is meeting."[18] Therefore, to meet God and truly live, we must die. Death is the maturest form of meeting, as meeting is the maturest face of death.

SEX AND DEATH

We can see this by using Freud's suggestive schema of the three stages of childhood development: oral, anal, and genital.[19] In each stage we find our identity in a different *hole,* a different doorway in our body, a different openness to the world outside. In the oral stage, the baby is dependent on his mother's breast, and identifies himself with his organ of sucking, his mouth. In the anal stage, independence begins with toilet training and the infant's realization that he can create something ("the anal product") from within all by himself. This is the stage of "the terrible twos" and their two magical discoveries: "me" and "no." Finally, the genital stage fully arises in puberty; its theme is relationship and love, meeting with the other, the sexually differentiated.

We have three different senses of oneness, or unity, in the three stages. In the oral stage, it is the cosmic oneness of "the oceanic feeling": the nature mystic's sense of oneness with the All, the cosmic mother. In the anal stage, it is the oneness of the ego, the independent individual—"I did it my way." In the genital stage, it is the oneness of "us"—"the two become one."[20]

It is in the genital stage that the four connected concepts of self, sex, death, and meeting take on their true significance. Self is now seen not as an isolated atom but as relational, as *for* meeting. The completest meeting, the most total and inclusive human relationship, is marriage. In marriage, sex becomes fully personal and the person becomes fully sexual; self and sex are married and meet. And when the sense of sexuality dawns, so does the sense of mortality. We seek sexual propagation, consciously or unconsciously, to overcome death. Sex and death are connected in nature too: sexless organisms like the cancer cell or the amoeba are immortal; sex arises only with mortality. Sexual reproduction is nature's trick to out-fox death; the species is preserved, though the individual dies.

Love (*amor*) and death (*morte*) are connected in language because they are connected in nature. The male bee dies after fertilizing the queen. The female preying mantis bites off the head of the male as he copulates, and death throes join copulatory spasms to make the thrusts stronger. Once inseminated, the female eats the male. The myths too relate the act of sexual love to dying: giving up the self, surrender in spirit as well as body, is necessary for the spontaneity of orgasm. Orgasm is a symbol of death and resurrection, as baptism is, a daring leap into nonbeing in the hope of new being.

But this is only the natural face of death, and of love. Free choice, individuality, and the meeting, or interpersonal relationship they make possible, are more than ingredients in nature; they are ingredients in us, and we are more than nature: we are spirit. The deepest meaning of sex is spiritual; sex is for meeting.

HOW DO YOU MEET DEATH?

Meeting is what individuality and free choice are for. I am an individual and I am free so that I can meet. Death is individual and death is free *so that death can be meeting*. Only free individuals can meet. Atoms and weather formations do not meet; they bump, merge, mangle, mesh, or mingle, but they do not meet. (Often, people act like atoms or weather formations.)

Death's meaning is up to the free choice of the individual because what death is to me depends on how I meet it. St. Augustine says:

> Of the first and bodily death we may say that it is good to the good and evil to the evil. . . . But a question not to be shirked arises: Whether in truth death is good to the good. For if it be, how has it come to pass that such a thing should be the punishment for sin? For the first men would not have suffered death had they not sinned. How then can that be good to the good which could not have happened except to the evil? . . . The Law is indeed good, because it is the prohibition of sin, and death is evil because it is the wages of sin; but as wicked men make an evil use not only of evil, but also of good things, so the righteous make a good use not only of good, but also of evil things. Whence it comes to pass that wicked make an ill use of the Law, though the Law is good, and that the good die well, though death is an evil.[21]

Socrates too knew that "no evil can ever happen to a good man, whether living or dead."[22] What death is, depends on how we meet it. Death is "good to the good, evil to the evil," victory to the victorious, hope to the hopeful, fear to the fearful, despair to the despairing. Two opposite attitudes toward death—victory and defeat—are mentioned in the New Testament. The first is 1 Corinthians 15:34-35: "Death is swallowed up in victory. O Death, where is thy victory? O Death, where is thy sting?" St. Paul taunts, mocks, sneers and jeers at death like a little child thumbing his nose—"Nyaa nyaa nyaa nyaa, nyaa nyaa!" The second is Hebrews 2:15, which speaks of "those who through fear of death were subjected to lifelong bondage." The fear of death casts a spell of bondage, uneasiness, and fear over a whole lifetime. There behind all the flowers is the same grinning skull. But "no evil can happen to a good man, whether living or dead." Even death has no sting. For a Christian, the answer to Paul's taunt, "O Death, where is thy sting?" is a simple and dramatic one: it is in the body of Jesus on the cross. Death cannot harm me because it is a stingless bee; its stinger is lodged in Christ.

MEETING LIGHT

At death we meet light, the light of absolute truth. The "being of light" reported by many resuscitated patients always asks a question, the same sort of question: Who are you? or What have you done with your life? or Are you ready to die? "And there is no possibility whatever either of misunderstanding or lying to the light."[23] Naturally, he is the one who has "searched me and known me,"[24] one to whom all thoughts lie bare and open."[25]

This meeting is a choice. We can choose or refuse the light. "This is how condemnation works: that though the light has come . . . men chose darkness rather than light."[26]

The questioner is God, I AM, the subject. The questioned object is man, the created image. Man cannot reverse this relationship. There is no hope in religion if religion means man's search for God. It is a natural and perennial search, but whatever man finds by this perennial search is an object of his finding, therefore an object, therefore not the true God, I AM, the absolute subject. But there is hope for God's search for man. Like light, God appears only to make *us* appear; He appears as the questioner not the questioned. He doesn't give Job a single answer to his dozens of excellent questions, but instead asks Job the primary question: Who do you think you are?

> Then the Lord answered Job out of the whirlwind:
> "Who is this that darkens counsel by words without knowledge?
> Gird up your loins like a man,
>   I will question you, and you will declare to me.
> Where were you when I laid the foundations of the earth?
>   Tell me, if you have understanding.[27]

Man cannot meet God—in life or in death—but God can meet man—in life and in death. When God meets us as questioner, as light, the choice is ours. God is always seeking, but we do not always choose to be found. Elihu says to Job:

> Why do you rail at Him
>   for not replying to you, word for word?
> God speaks first in one way,
>   and then in another, but no one notices.[28]

We do not hear God when we are busy speaking. God shows up only when we shut up. Job's best words are his last, "The words of Job are ended." [29] *Then* God appears. He says, "Be still and know that I am God." [30] And we reply: "No, God, *You* be still and know that I am me!"

Why do we do this? Because we do not *want* to be found most of the time. That is why the object-God is so much more comfortable than the subject-God; that is why God's search for man upsets us, as man's search for God does not:

> Men are reluctant to pass over from the notion of an abstract and negative deity to the living God. I do not wonder. Here lies the deepest tap-root of Pantheism and of the objection to traditional imagery. It was hated not, at bottom, because it pictured Him as man but because it pictured Him as king, or even as warrior. The Pantheist's God does nothing, demands nothing. He is there if you wish for Him, like a book on a shelf. He will not pursue you. There is no danger that at any time heaven and earth should flee away at His glance. If He were the truth, then we could really say that all the Christian images of kingship were a historical accident of which our religion ought to be cleansed. It is with a shock that we discover them to be indispensable. You have had a shock like that before, in connection with smaller matters—when the line pulls at your hand, when something breathes beside you in the darkness. So here; the shock comes at the precise moment when the thrill of *life* is communicated to us along the clue we have been following. It is always shocking to meet life where we thought we were alone. "Look out!" we cry, "it's *alive*." And therefore this is the very point at which so many draw back—I would have done so myself if I could—and proceed no further with Christianity. An "impersonal God"—well and good. A subjective God of beauty, truth and goodness, inside our own heads—better still. A formless life-force surging through us, a vast power which we can tap—best of all. But God Himself, alive, pulling at the other end of the cord, perhaps approaching at an infinite speed, the hunter, king, husband—that is quite another matter. There comes a moment when the children who have been playing at burglars hush suddenly: was that a *real* footstep in the hall? There comes a moment when people who have been dabbling in religion ("Man's search for God"!) suddenly draw back. Supposing we really found Him? We never meant it to come to *that!* Worse still, supposing He had found us?
>
> So it is a sort of Rubicon. One goes across; or not.[31]

The ultimate meeting is the ultimate choice.

JUDGMENT

The meeting is also judgment. The meeting is not merely the *occasion* for judgment; it *is* the the judgment. For this judgment is not an external sentence meted out to me, but simply the truth of myself now exposed to the inescapable light of God.

This judgment is not a matter of degree but is absolute, since the light is absolute. What I am is a relative thing in every way but one. "There's a little good in the worst of us and a little bad in the best of us, so it ill becomes the best of us to speak ill of the worst of us." But in one way what I am is absolute: 'to be or not to be, that is the question.'[32] Either I am or not; either I have life or not; either I was born or not. This one thing—life or death—this one absolute, is the object of God's judgment. But it is not my physical life that is judged; that has died. It is my spiritual life or death.

Once spiritual life is present, there are degrees of spiritual health, as there are degrees of physical health. But spiritual *life,* like physical life, is not a matter of degree, because it is not essentially a matter of actions, good deeds, brownie points, but of my being. My actions have merited a 70, say, or a 7, on God's grading scale. But my being merits either a "real" or an "unreal," either an "I know you" or an "I never knew you."[33] God does not grade on a curve but on pass/fail. There is no sliding scale and no cutoff point. How terribly unfair any cutoff point would be, say, Heaven at 70 and Hell at 69.9, or heaven at 7 and hell at 6.99. With God, the passing grade is zero, and to pass is sheer gift.

I once dreamed I died and stood before the gates of heaven. God asked me, "Why should I let you in here? This place is only for *experts.*" I was so confused that I blurted out, "Well—I'm a pretty good chess player." He replied, "Not nearly good enough; not an expert." I said, "I try to be a good husband and father." He said, "Sorry, only experts need apply." I said, "I'm told I'm a good teacher." He said, "Not good enough; not an expert." I started shuffling off in despair when the light dawned. I ran back to the gate, rang the bell, and said to God when He came, "You have to let me in here. I'm an expert at something." He replied, "Oh yeah? What?" I said, "I'm an expert sinner. I've thought of millions of new and clever ways to sin. I really know what sin is. But I'm a sorry expert. Please forgive me." He said, "Well, it's about time you found out who this place is for! Welcome inside."

Forgiveness is a gift, and a gift must be both freely given and freely received in order to be a gift. If I offer you a thousand dollars and you do not take it, you do not have it, and my generosity avails you not a penny. The gift of eternal life that God offers is like a lover's gift of life, like a proposition. God propositions me, but He will not rape, only seduce. If I freely accept His proposal, I become pregnant with His Life; and no one is *partly* pregnant. That's why the judgment is not a matter of degree. There are only two kinds of people in the world; and they are not the good and the bad, but the living and the dead, the twice-born and the once-born, the children of God and the children of Adam, the pregnant and the barren. That is the difference between heaven and hell.

HEAVEN AND HELL

God's judgment reveals whether or not I am in heaven, that is, whether or not heaven is in me. The judgment does not send me to heaven or hell but reveals the presence of heaven or the absence of heaven (=hell) in my soul. This kingdom of heaven in the soul is like a seed, or a fetus now; death is its birth. Jesus sees paradise in the soul of the good thief on the cross and judges him: "Today (now) you are to be with Me in Paradise."[34] To the one with no heaven in his soul he says, "I never knew you." These are the most terrifying words ever spoken; for what God knows is real (He creates simply by knowing), and for me not to be known by God is for me not to be real. Hell is not just a lack of pleasure or even of goodness; it is a lack of being. It is not eternal life plus pain and badness; it is eternal *death.* "What is cast (casts itself) into hell is not a man; it is 'remains.'"[35]

In a classroom, the question is How good do you have to be to pass? In a meeting, the question is Do you love me? God's judgment is meeting. Therefore hell is a real possibility. One need not be spectacularly wicked; one need only say to God, "No thank you; I want only this—to say 'I did it my way.'" A little bit of hell from a typical student paper:

> Man turned to religion so that he could lean on an outside force. He was looking for a crutch, a father-figure. This I felt I did not need. I could make it on my own.

My comment on this was, "Do you think you will feel that way also when you die?"

There are "only two kinds of people in the end: those who say to God, 'Thy will be done,' and those to whom God says, in the end, '*thy* will be done.'"[36] Where God's will is done is where heaven is; for God's will is perfect joy. Wherever we let God's will be done on earth, we let the Kingdom of Heaven come, and fulfill our prayer: "Thy kingdom come, Thy will be done, on earth as it is in Heaven."

THE CONSUMMATION OF THE QUEST

Life is a quest. This is the basic image and basic plot of all stories; it is what makes even fairy tales "true to life." Death as rendezvous is the consummation of life as quest, life as pilgrimage. It is the fulfillment of our deepest, highest, craziest, and most wonderful desire, the desire for infinite joy. "Thou hast made us for Thyself, and (therefore) our hearts are restless until they rest in Thee."[37] "All your life an unattainable ecstasy has hovered just beyond the grasp of your consciousness. The day is coming when you will wake to find, beyond all hope, that you have attained it; or else, that it was within your grasp and you have lost it forever."[38] "All day long we are in some degree helping each other toward one or the other of these two destinations."[39]

This is it. This meeting, this spiritual intercourse with God, is the end of ends, the meaning of life, the supreme good, the *summum bonum,* the thing we desire in all that we desire. It is all truth, all goodness, and all beauty, and therefore all joy. All of life is foreplay, courtship, seduction. Only in death is the unendurably beautiful Beloved finally touched. The dying words of the Earl of Shaftesbury were: "I am touching the hem of His garment."

For this touch, God has brought me—how far? An infinite distance, from absolutely nothing, from nonbeing to being, through all the events of my life, just for this meeting. And He Himself has come an infinite distance—from infinity—to meet me. Two infinite distances, from nothing and from infinity, are overcome for the sake of this meeting. For this is the meaning of Life: "All real living is meeting."[40]

The Christian adds the ultimate reason and foundation in God for this meaning of human life: God in His very essence is not aloneness but meeting, not a mere individual but a society, not the oneness of sheer mathematical identity but the oneness of love. "God *is* love" only if God is more than one person; God is love only if God is a trinity of lover, beloved, and loving.

ULTIMATE MEANING OR ULTIMATE MEANINGLESSNESS

Death is the golden chariot sent by the Bridegroom to fetch his bride. The chariot moves exactly on its appointed rounds because love is exact. You, and no one else, are the bride; now, and no other time, is the moment of marriage. Death is no accident if love is no accident. Lovers do not stumble into each other's arms; love is *not* blind. Love has eyes; eyes that nothing else has. If God's love planned our birth and our life from all eternity, is it likely that He would leave our death to chance? He leads through the two great gateways.

Out of billions of possibilities, I, this unique *I,* came to be. Why? It's either a providential plot or an incomprehensible improbability. "Either we live by accident and die by accident, or we live by plan and die by plan," says Thornton Wilder. "Some say that . . . to the gods we are like the flies that boys kill on a summer day. And some say, on the contrary, that the very sparrows do not lose a feather that has not been brushed away by the finger of God." [41]

Nothing is more purposive than the thrust of the lover's glance, his kiss, his proposal, and his impregnation. A kiss is meaning incarnate, pure sign. The thrust of the husband's organ into the wife's body is not merely a machine for pleasure; it is heavy with meaning, with plan and purpose and intention. This is an image of death. Death is the ripping of the earthly hymen by the heavenly phallus, the consummation not only of joy but also of meaning and purpose:

> This is the moment for which I have been secretly waiting during my whole life. I now utter the one word of which my love is still capable and which sums up my whole life, the dreams of mankind and the longing of the universe: "Thou." Out of that word there grows an eternal embrace. Out of the mighty destiny of Death I make a personal decision of love. . . .
>
> This is God's moment. He thought of this moment already billions of years ago when he created the world. He thought of it at every stage of the slowly ascending evolution of the world. He thought of it when he prepared his own coming, during the time he spent as a stranger, forsaken and unnoticed in a remote corner of our world. He thought of it during his terrible agony, in his death; in his descent, in what we call the descent into

hell, when he entered into the heart of the world; in his resurrection and ascension, in which he filled the universe.

He went through all that and took it on himself, so that I might meet him, now in death . . . and utter the word full of love: "Thou." Saying "thou" then snatches me out of my nothingness and creates new being in me. . . .

Death is truly the peak of world-events, the source of eternal life. In it man plunges more steeply than can be conceived into unfathomable depths, but only in order to mount up again and surge over, like a rising breaker, into eternal consummation.[42]

IF DEATH IS SO GREAT, WHY NOT SUICIDE?

Why not suicide? Because death is not a good in itself but an evil in itself. It is our enemy. But God uses it by nature as our friend, by resurrection as our mother, and by this meeting as our lover. Its first face does not disappear when we see its other faces, but it is *aufgehoben*, taken up, transformed, integrated into and used by a greater face. The evil, used by the good, becomes good:

> Like an artist who is able to make use of a fault or an impurity in the stone he is sculpting or the bronze he is casting so as to produce more exquisite lines or a more beautiful tone, God, without sparing us the partial deaths, nor the final death, which form an essential part of our lives, transfigures them by integrating them in a better plan—*provided we lovingly trust in him.*[43]

Just as "the corruption of the best is the worst" *(corruptio optimi pessima)*, the redemption of the worst is the best *(redemptio pessimi optima)*. Christians call man's greatest crime, the decide, "*Good* Friday" because it effects the salvation of the world! The instrument is evil, but its power is used, against its will, for good. God practices a kind of judo, turning the opponent's own strongest force and momentum against him.

Let us enter more deeply into this incredible divine judo. (Belief is not required, just imagination—another little thought experiment.) Let us imagine the Devil's fiendish joy at the folly of the Incarnation. How foolish, smirks Satan, is God's love! it leads Him into the great tactical mistake of leaving His impregnable Heaven. In order to redeem the mankind God loves, He must become a man, enter enemy-occupied territory, become subject to the conditions of "the ruler of this world."[44] The ruler inspires a few of his key agents and He is crucified. Imagine the delicious taste in Satan's mouth as he savors the unthinkable pain of the death of God, a death not only in body but in spirit, a death that is hell. Imagine how Satan relishes forever those unthinkably terrible words: "My God, my God, why hast Thou forsaken me?" Victory! Satan has killed God, split the eternal Trinity, introduced the separation of death into ultimate reality, and proved the utter folly and defeat of God's love for Man. And precisely *this* is Satan's ultimate defeat and God's victory; precisely this death is the instrument of man's salvation from death and from Satan! Imagine Satan's utter consternation, astonishment, terror, and resentment at being used by the divine judo!

But though evil is used for good, this is no excuse for evil. "Offenses must come, but woe unto him by whom they come."[45] "Where sin abounded, grace did much more abound. . . . What shall we say then? Shall we continue in sin, that grace may abound? God forbid."[46] Though Judas' betrayal and the crucifixion brought about salvation, Judas was not saved by it. Though our death is used by God for our good, *we* may not use it: "thou shalt not kill."[47] Death is the divine surgeon's knife, not to be used except by the Great Physician. Only one can wield the sacred sword Excalibur: the One who sits in the Seige Perilous, the chair in which only the King can sit.

PRAYER AND DEATH

Not suicide but prayer is the way to practice death in life. Prayer is a rehearsal for death; prayer is a little death. For to pray is essentially to enter God's presence, and to enter God's presence, we must die: "No man can see My face and live."[48]

This is a blessed death; we die to our own presence, our own I AM. We stop being our own God and "let God be God."[49] Sartre is right—man's essential desire is to be God. The practice of the presence of God, which is the essence of prayer, dies to this desire, to the self-idol that claims to be God and to the world that is a function of that idol, "*my* world." Only when we die to the desire to be our own God, our own Father, the attempt to father ourselves—only then can we be fathered by God. When we refuse the Oedipus complex, we are "born of God."

Prayer is incredibly simple. The only essential step is the first step, dying. Dying to myself and my world, giving up self and world and all the things self could be doing in the world instead of praying, giving up the claim to ownership of self and world. My self is my will; once I say to God, "My will is Yours; Your will be done"—once I say that, the rest of the prayer prays itself, for it is not mine but God's. The reason our prayers are not answered is that they are *our* prayers. *His* will is always done. His prayers are always answered.

Prayer is an affirmation of our creaturely role as feminine, as wooed, as impregnated, as responder to the divine initiative. Prayer is our response-ability instead of our ability. We do not initiate prayer; God does. God continually proposes to us "Will you be with Me now?" And we usually respond "No, I will be with myself; I will practice spiritual masturbation instead of spiritual intercourse." But when we weary of this emptiness, we turn ("repent," "con-vert") to God, and He fills us.

Prayer is the preparation for the last turning to God, for death. Perhaps everything that takes us out of ourselves is a preparation for death; love, music, and the honest pursuit of truth come to mind. But prayer is the best preparation for death because in it we are not only taken out of ourselves but also into the presence of God. Prayer is heaven on earth.

"I'M SO HAPPY I COULD DIE!"

What do we mean by these mysterious words? Some great secret lies hidden in them, and it is the same secret as the secret of prayer. We say these words only when we feel Joy, that deep happiness that is more than happiness. It is "ecstasy," *ek-stasis,* standing-outside-oneself, self-forgetfulness. At its least, this is simply interest, fascination with something other; at its height, it is the thrill of becoming nothing in God: "Blow, blow, blow till I be/ But the breath of the Spirit blowing in me."[50] People have not really lived if they have not died that death, if "they have never felt homesickness for something unknown and far away, nor the depth which consists in being nothing at all."[51]

This is not masochism, the lowest and most degraded form of love, but love's very highest and purest form, of which its lowest form is an ape. It is the gift of self:

The self is given to us that we may sacrifice it; it is ours that we, like Christ, may have something to offer—not that we should torment it [= masochism], but that we should deny it; not that we should cross it, but that we should abandon it utterly: then it can no more be vexed. "What can this mean?— we are not to thwart, but to abandon?" It means this: we must refuse, abandon, deny self altogether as a ruling or determining or originating element in us. It is to be no longer the regent of our action. We are no more to think "What should I like to do?" but "What would the Living One have me to do?"[52]

This is union with God, oneness of the divine and human wills. It is our ultimate destiny, and the door to it is resurrection. But the door to resurrection is death. That is why we secretly desire death. Physical death is the door to the door to spiritual death and consummation. Death is our lover, death fulfills our being, because we are snakes destined to shed our skins, caterpillars destined to live again as butterflies by dying as caterpillars. The secret hidden in "I'm so happy I could die" is our secret caterpillar-knowledge of death, believing in the butterfly.

LOVE IS STRONGER THAN DEATH

Amor vincit omnia, say the poets: Love conquers all.[53] Does this mean it conquers even death? The poets say that it does, that love is stronger than death.[54] But what does this mean? It means that when love and death meet, it is death that is changed, not love. When the flood of love meets the dam of death, it is not stopped by the dam. Not only does it sweep away the dam, but it sweeps the dam along its waters, it transforms the dam into a part of itself. Love is so much stronger than death that it makes death into a lover.

Marcel calls death "the test of presence."[55] Presence is not merely physical; stones are not present to each other, nor are sleeping bodies. Nor is presence merely mental; the presence of a mental picture or memory image is not a real presence, not the presence of a person. When we are really present to each other, I am literally a part of you and you of me—literally, but not physically. I am a part of your spiritually. But this does not mean merely mentally; as we have just seen, mental presence is not yet real presence. What *does* it mean then? What presence means is most clearly brought out by death. Death re-

moves physical presence but not presence. St. Augustine's meditation
on the death of his friend shows this:

> My heart was black with grief. Whatever I looked on had the air of
> death. My native place was a prison-house and my home a strange unhappi-
> ness. The things we had done together became sheer torment without him.
> My eyes were restless looking for him, but he was not there. I hated all
> places because he was not in them. They could not say: 'He will come soon,'
> as they would in his life when he was absent. I became a great enigma to
> myself and I was forever asking my soul why it was sad and why it disquiet-
> ed me so sorely. And my soul did not know what to answer me. . . . I had no
> delight but in tears, for tears had taken the place my friend had had in the
> love of my heart.
>
> I was at once utterly weary of life and in great fear of death. It may be
> that the more I loved him the more I hated and feared, as the cruellest en-
> emy, that death which had taken him from me; and I was filled with the
> thought that it might snatch away any man as suddenly as it had snatched
> him. . . . I wondered that other mortals should live when he was dead whom
> I had loved as if he would never die; and I marvelled still more that he
> should be dead and I his other self living still. Rightly has a friend been
> called "the half of my soul." For I thought of my soul and his soul as one
> soul in two bodies, and my life was a horror to me because I would not live
> halved.[56]

"I would not live halved"—like a ghost or a corpse, the two staples of
horror movies, though no one has ever been harmed by either. They
are horrible because they are the two halves of us, separated by death.
Friends are also the two halves of a composite self, "a new creation,"
an "us." Friendship, like all love, really creates a new reality, not just
an I who loves plus a Thou who is loved but an *us*. That most ordinary
of words suddenly becomes extraordinarily magical through friendship
and love. Does death conquer this us-ness? Is death stronger than love?
Death is the test of presence, of us-ness, of love.

Grief like Augustine's proves that a friend is literally a part of my
soul. If it were not so, if I were only myself, if each individual's identity
extended not to all those he "identified with" or "found his identity in"
but only to his own self, his own skin, his own epidermis (this is "epidermiolatry," idolatry of the epidermis), then there would be no intelli-
gible explanation for grief, for the cause-and-effect relationship between the external, physical event in the world (the friend's death) and
the internal, emotional event in me (grief), between the beat of his

heart stopping and the beat of mine nearly stopping. In order for there to be a relationship of cause and effect, there must be a continuum, a common medium. The cause and the effect must touch each other; they must be present to each other. Billiard balls move each other only on the same surface; predicates modify subjects only in the same sentence. My friend's soul is not outside me, as his body is; it is "my other self." Death and grief reveal this, the mystery of love, "the two becoming one" spirit.

Love is stronger than death, for death is the test of presence and love meets the test. C.S. Lewis writes about his wife's death:

> If H. is not now, then she never was. I mistook a cloud of atoms for a person. There aren't, and never were, any people. Death only reveals the vacuity that was always there. What we call the living are simply those who have not yet been unmasked. All equally bankrupt, but some not yet declared.[57]

If this is true, says the knight in Bergman's *The Seventh Seal,*

> "Then life is an outrageous horror. No one can live in the face of death, knowing that all is nothingness."[58]

Whatever our beliefs, we want to refuse absence and affirm presence:

> I was a little child when the news came of my father's death, far away. That night, as usual, I prayed for him. But my aunt stopped me. "Darling," she said, "you must not pray for Father now; it is wrong." And I can remember still how I shrank back, feeling as if someone had slammed the door and shut Father outside.[58]

Love cannot tolerate absence. Death seems to be absence, but love is stronger than death.

Death is not absence but presence in relation to the earthly beloved because death is not absence but presence in relation to God, the Giver of all earthly beloveds. "Thou hast made Death glorious and triumphant; for through its portals we enter into the Presence of the Living God."[59] God makes death work backwards: absence becomes presence, separation becomes union.

The face of death and darkness becomes the face of life and light. The facade of the abyss becomes the facade of home. Death has five faces, and God has an infinity of faces, but the last face of death is the first face of God.

THE END

Here is the last mystery of death. We have looked at each face, and now we find who it is that wears all the faces. It's good old God!

It's either God or nothingness. Death asks the ultimate question, to which only two answers are possible. The ultimate reality is known at the ultimate moment of death, and it is either being or nothingness, ultimate meaning or ultimate meaninglessness. Either God wears the mask of death, or death wears the mask of God.

If it is really God behind all the masks of death, what happens when a person dies? Exactly the opposite of what seems to happen. The eye does not grow dim but bright. Death does not approach; death recedes forever. Life does not ebb but flows over our old container, overcomes it, kills it. It is not a defect of life but an excess of life that kills us. Death seems to catch up with us from behind, from our past, from the aging process built into our material bodies. But it is life that catches up with us from ahead and kills this body of death. We think the opposite because we look from the past. From the past, we see what was, that is, the body of death and its process of aging and dying. God sees from ahead, from what to us is future. What to us will be, to Him is. From God's point of view—the true point of view—it is His eternal life in the form of our heavenly body, our spiritual body, meeting our body of death at the point of death that slays and conquers this body. Our own new body kills our old body. Our new body is the sword in God's hand by which He executes judgment upon our old body. And the ultimate meaning of this execution, the ultimate meaning of death, is love. Our old body is our hymen; God is the phallic sword; and our body succumbs to death because we are ravished by our Lover.

CONCLUDING UNSCIENTIFIC POSTSCRIPT

It is only a thought experiment, but it may become for any one a faith experiment. Faith is an experiment, like love; it is not merely a hypothesis, or even a belief. It is the accepting of the divine proposal of marriage.

No one by now will have missed the obvious point that our thought experiment is essentially the Christian faith experiment. The essence of Christianity is extremely simple: in Christ God appears as our lover, who asks our free permission to impregnate us with His eternal life, and faith is our "yes" to that proposal.

"Yes" is a simple word, and a single word. Love, like death, stills our busy tongues. In their rapturous embraces lovers do not talk, only sigh with joy. The last word is silence. The silence of love is not empty but full, too full for words, overflowing our thimble-sized words with an ocean-sized life. The best words for that life and that love that are stronger than death are not our words but God's:

> In that day, says the Lord, you will call me, "my husband," and no longer will you call me "my Baal" (my idol). . . . And I will betroth you to Me for ever; I will betroth you to Me in righteousness and in justice, in steadfast love and in mercy. I will betroth you to Me in faithfulness *(emeth)*; and you shall know the Lord.[60]
>
> Then I heard what seemed to be the voice of a great multitude, like the sound of many waters and like the sound of mighty thunderpeals, crying: "Hallelujah! For the Lord our God the Almighty reigns. Let us rejoice and exult and give Him the glory, for the marriage of the Lamb has come, and His Bride has made herself ready." . . . And the angel said to me, "Write this: Blessed are those that are invited to the marriage supper of the Lamb."[61]
>
> I Jesus have sent my angel ("messenger") to you with this testimony for the churches. I am the root and the offspring of David, the bright morning star. The Spirit and the Bride say, "Come." And let him who hears say, "Come." And let him who is thirsty come, let him who desires take the water of life without price.[62]

NOTES

1. Shakespeare, *Measure for Measure,* act 3, scene 1.
2. *Song of Songs* 5:8–11; 6:8–9.
3. Exod. 3:13–14.
4. John 8:58.
5. Martin Heidegger, *Being and Time,* (New York: Harper & Row, 1962), p. 284.
6. See C.S. Lewis, *The Four Loves* (London: Collins Fontana Books, 1960).
7. Matt. 10:39.
8. George MacDonald, quoted in C.S. Lewis, *George MacDonald: An Anthology,* (New York: Macmillan, 1978) no. 129, p. 57–58.
9. Jean-Paul Sartre, *Being and Nothingness: An Essay on Phenomenological Ontology* (New York: Philosophical Library, 1956), pp. 60–67.

10. Op. cit., pp. 471–534; See Gabriel Marcel, "Existence and Human Freedom" in *The Philosophy of Existentialism* (Secaucus, N.J.: Citadel Press, 1956), pp. 74–76.

11. See Sigmund Freud, *Beyond the Pleasure Principle,* trans. James Strachey (New York: Liveright Publishing Corp., 1950) and *The Ego and the Id,* trans. Joan Riviere (London: Hogarth Press, 1950).

12. Peter Kreeft, "Johnny, jnana-yoga, and Jehovah", Proceedings of the American Catholic Philosophical Association, New England Regional Convention, 1969.

13. *Song of Songs* 1:2; 1:4; 2:7. Italics mine.

14. Deut. 30:19.

15. Matt. 25:40.

16. T.S. Eliot, "The Hollow Men," in *Collected Poems.*

17. Søren Kierkegaard, *Philosophical Fragments,* trans. David Swenson (Princeton, N.J.: Princeton University Press, 1936), ch. 2, sec. A.

18. Martin Buber, *I And Thou,* trans. Walter Kaufmann (New York: Charles Scribner's Sons, 1970), p. 62. Compare the Ronald Gregor Smith translation.

19. Sigmund Freud, *An Outline of Psychoanalysis,* trans. James Strachey (New York: W.W. Norton, 1949), pp. 9–12; See also *Three Contributions to the Theory of Sex,* trans. A.A. Brill (New York: Dutton, 1950), pp. 57–60 *et passim.* Freud's fourth stage, the genital, has its beginnings in his third stage, the phallic; the three-stage dialectic of dependence vs. independence resolved in love, therefore, is Freudian.

20. Gen. 2:24.

21. Augustine *The City of God* bk. 13, chs. 2, 3, 5.

22. Plato *The Apology of Socrates* 41cd.

23. Raymond Moody, *Life After Life* (New York: Bantam Books, 1976), p. 60.

24. Ps. 139:1.

25. Heb. 4:12–13.

26. John 3:19 (Jerusalem Bible).

27. Job 38:1–4.

28. Job 33:13–14 (Jerusalem Bible).

29. Job 31:40.

30. Psalm 46:10.

31. C.S. Lewis, *Miracles,* (New York: Macmillan, 1955), pp. 113–114.

32. Shakespeare, *Hamlet,* act 3, scene 1, line 56.

33. Matt. 7:23.

34. Luke 23:43.

35. C. S. Lewis, *The Problem of Pain,* (New York: Macmillan, 1962), p. 125.

36. C. S. Lewis, *The Great Divorce* (New York: Macmillan, 1946), p. 72.

37. Augustine *Confessions* 1. 1.

38. Lewis, *Problem of Pain,* p. 148.

39. C. S. Lewis, "The Weight of Glory," in *The Weight of Glory and Other Addresses* (New York: Macmillan, 1949), p. 15.

40. Martin Buber, *I And Thou.*

41. Thornton Wilder, *The Bridge of San Luis Rey* (New York: A.& C. Boni, 1928), pp. 19, 23.

42. Ladislaus Boros, "Death: A Theological Reflection," in *The Mystery of Suffering and Death,* ed. Michael Taylor, S.J., pp. 177–178.

43. Pierre Teilhard de Chardin, *The Divine Milieu,* (New York: Harper & Row, 1960), p. 86.

44. John 12:31, 14:30, 16:11.

45. Matt. 18:7.

46. Rom. 5:20; 6:1.

47. Exod. 20:13.
48. Exod. 33:20.
49. See Jean-Paul Sartre, *Existentialism and Human Emotions* (New York: Philosophical Library, 1957), p. 65.
50. "Spirit of God," unpublished hymn by Sister Miriam Theresa Winter.
51. Søren Kierkegaard, *Journals,* 1837, July 14 [*A Kierkegaard Anthology,* ed. Robert Bretall (Princeton, N.J.: Princeton University Press, 1946), p. 9].
52. George MacDonald quoted in Lewis, *George MacDonald,* no. 157, p. 72.
53. Virgil *Eclogues* 10. 69; Dryden, *Pastoral* 10 *Gallus.*
54. *Song of Songs* 8:7.
55. Gabriel Marcel, "On the Ontological Mystery," in *The Philosophy of Existentialism,* trans. Manya Harari (New York: Citadel Press, 1956), p. 37.
56. Augustine *Confessions* 4. 4–6.
57. C. S. Lewis, *A Grief Observed* (New York: Seabury Press, 1963), pp. 32–33.
58. Ingmar Bergman, "The Seventh Seal," in *Four Screenplays of Ingmar Bergman,* trans. Lars Malmstrom and David Kushner (New York: Simon & Schuster, 1960), p. 150.
58. J. Paterson Smyth, *The Gospel of the Hereafter* (out of print).
59. From a choral anthem, "Open Our Eyes" by Jean Pasquet and William Charles McFarland.
60. Hos. 2:16, 19–20.
61. Rev. 19:6–7, 9.
62. Rev. 22:16–17.

Six Scenes from a Close Encounter with the Dark Angel

Because "he jests at scars who never felt a wound," and because the dimension of personal experience might be thought to be conspicuous by its absence, I include here after much hesitation these candid excerpts from my personal diary written in the hospital where my wife and I suddenly found ourselves confronting a brain tumor in our five-year-old daughter. The book was written before this "close encounter," not as a result of it. I include it simply as my other half: the book is my mind, this is my guts.

I

The first vision that burns unforgettably in my mind is the simple one of a locked door: the back door of our house. As my wife and I left that morning for the hospital tests that would show what was wrong with our daughter, a small, dark insect in my mind buzzed with worry. Our pediatrician had seen pressure in the back of her eyes that made him insist on an immediate appointment with a neurologist; and that was scary, even though her symptoms before the examination didn't seem terribly serious to us: poor morning appetite, naps, a dislike of gym, clumsy balance. The thought "brain tumor" did not now escape us, but that thought seemed somehow foreign and incredible. But as I locked the back door of the house the thought pulled at my mind: Are you locking away the first half of your life today? Will you ever again in all of time return to this same house? Or will it be a totally different house, a different place in a different world? And when you return, will you be the same person, or will someone else who only looks like you open this door? Someone who looks alive but is really partly dead, a bit of a ghost, a wraith, a member of the kingdom of the dead? My precious daughter, my perfect one, if you are dying, so am I.

A second vision has the same meaning. It is a place on the highway, a junction, the place the turnpike begins that carries us into the city where she will have more tests. Shall I ever be able to pass that junction again without remembering? The thought was a knife, and it cut both my wife and me at the same time at the same place on the highway. Will the world ever be the same again? Are we turning a corner on our life's road that is a one-way street?

"You can't go home again" because when you come back, the rest of the world has made a half turn in the mean time. The night falls; suppose there is no dawn?

II

Strange how the mind fixates on physical details in order to handle the unhandleable. When we can't handle truth we handle facts. We miniaturize; we find some small objective correlative to associate with the unhandleably enormous subjective feeling. In this case it is the chair I was sitting in when the doctor came out of the CAT-scan room with the results of the computerized head X rays, while my wife was still in the X-ray room with my daughter. I will always remember the exact spot each chair leg occupied in the room. I will also remember the look on the doctor's face—an embarrassed look, a look not at me but vaguely around me, as if looking for help. It was as if he, not I, were the sufferer, or as if he were responsible for the bad news, the "blame the messenger" syndrome. But I could not blame the messenger; he seemed no more comfortable delivering the message than I in receiving it.

Large brain tumor. What does that mean? Well, of course, this is not final or official; you will have to talk to Doctor so and so, I'm only a resident. Tell me everything you know; I have to know. It is cancerous? We can't be sure until we go in. Can it be removed? We don't know; even if it isn't malignant, it could be in the brain stem, inoperable. Facts, please, statistics. (When we can't take truth, we feed on facts.) Well, if it's inoperable, the life expectancy is from nine months to two to five years. And those years would be a gradual deterioration? Yes; but pain killers could make it painless . . . such a beautiful child- . . . what a shame.

Suddenly, instead of forty pounds of life, I confronted forty pounds of death. No one on earth can prepare you for the feeling. It sounds terrible to say it, but now that it is all over, I am grateful for having been allowed to experience that horrible, hopeless feeling, the worst moment of my life. A sudden vision of months of irreversible degeneration, slow dying, with neither her nor us understanding why. Dying is harder to bear than death, and the dying of a child infinitely harder than the dying of the old. I knew then what despair was. It is not a thought, not even a feeling. It exists not in the brain or even the heart but in the stomach. I tasted despair in the gut. My stomach suddenly turned to mud and iron. The round world swooped away, fell into the lightless abyss like a trillion-ton stone. It seemed to drop out of my guts. My mud-and-iron stomach was somehow identical with that world, dropping an infinite distance, becoming incalculably remote and utterly inaccessible. Both world and guts dropped away from my eyes, my head, my mind: the knowledge of the truth. The truth could not be both known and felt at the same time. I had to split in half. If the truth had to be felt with the iron-and-mud gut, the same truth could not be accepted by the clear, thin light of the mind. For about two minutes I knew death as a stranger as a desperate reaction to death as an enemy, I knew the protective shell of withdrawal, a sanity-saving retreat from unbearable truth. This can't possibly be really happening to us. It's a bad dream. I can wake up in a minute, and it will all have gone away. The real world can't possibly be like that; it would be too absurd.

In that feeling, I am convinced, there is more than mere denial of death (though there is, of course, denial); there is also an affirmation. An affirmation that meaning and sense and goodness reign at the heart of reality, rather than absurdity. The "real world" didn't appear now as the heart of reality, as it usually does. Not that it was unreal, illusory; but that it was a surface, not the depths. There in the depths, at the bottom line, at the heart of all things, in the final analysis death and dying and doom and despair cannot be the truth, not the final truth. They are not illusions, but they are not truth either: they are masks.

It is a quite unverifiable assurance to anyone else; but to the one who knows it, it is beyond the need for verification. It is self-verifying. It is more than a wish, or even a hope; it is a prophetic *fiat,* an imperial absolute, a categorical imperative. For it is uttered by love. Love insists that contrary to appearances life holds the strings even of death. Our daughter may be dying; the affirmation does not insist that she is not, as denial does. But it does insist that her dying is not her last word, the last truth.

This affirmation does not feel at all like an illusion or a defense mechanism, a denial of the truth; but precisely like an affirmation of the truth, a genuine insight into objective reality. In the face of the visible triumph of death, it proclaims an invisible kingdom. The ground of this proclamation is not my desires or even my beliefs but my seeing: some deep inner eye that remained in the very center of my being when my head and my guts fell apart, and that kept me together. It was neither the head nor the guts that knew this, it was ME—center, heart, depth. Love comes from there; it was love that knew and affirmed her undying being.

But my guts meanwhile wanted to defecate. A perfect symbol, though a grotesque one. The physical dying was like stool, a true thing but a thing to be exuded from the living self, from the perfect body: "Death, thou shalt die." Death must be like that: the perfect immortal body putting away the used-up waste product of the mortal body, the living flushing away the dead.

But the dying body is there, and it is dying. Whether in two years or in ninety-two, it is dying. It makes no qualitative difference to the philosopher. But it makes a qualitative difference to the parent! Two years—in a flash, all their gut-wrenching sorrow, unendurable yet endured, all the hopeless details of a long and irreversible deterioration, passed in my imagination. And as it did, a piece of common sense assured me that there is a real reason why this can't happen to us. We are not saints or heroes. We are cowards. We can't take this, and you get only what you can take. God may take us to the brink; but He will not take us over it. He will not let us fall.

Then the rational doubts chattered: won't He? Don't you see some go over the brink? And the deeper mind answered, Ah, but that is not the question. You have no assurances about anyone else, only yourself. Each has his own assurance because each has his own self and his own life. But, spoke the doubt, why couldn't He let you slip through His fingers? Because, triumphantly retorted the assurance, you *are* one of His fingers.

Yes, death is a mother and a lover, death is God's loving touch. My mind did not doubt this; it knew. But my feelings were weak, vacillating and uncertain in their trust. And my guts remained utterly unredeemed; they threatened to pull my mind and feelings down with them into the abyss together with that trillion ton stone that was my guts' world. The assurance was as far from my guts as I was from that stone falling away into the abyss, too far for my reach ever again to touch it.

"It" is not an *it,* it is you, my precious one, my baby. Where are you going? On what far, dark, and empty seas do you wander? Why can't I come with you? Where am I without you, with this you-shaped emptiness in me instead? Which of us is nowhere? How far is that from home?

III

She was allowed to come home for a day or two before being hospitalized for the operation. It was like a prisoner's last meal. We took her shopping for toys, for pajamas for the hospital, for dozens of infinitely precious little things, as the thought constantly tortured us to dry tears: Is this her last this? Her last that? We tried to make what might be her last normal day perfect. Today she can have whatever she wants. We know the books say this is wrong; but the books don't have a daughter who may be dying.

Our other children don't understand why we're so preoccupied and silent on this vacationlike shopping day. They know of the operation, but not of the nearness to death. We buy them special treats too, of course, and we worry about them too. Did we do right by them? (The dying of one and the thoughts it gives rise to seem somehow to envelop all.) Did we put second things first and first things second? Did we disobey the fundamental ethical imperative; did we love things and use people instead of vice versa? Did we forget that the things that seem to our senses to change and grow and move so quickly—our children— are really the solid, eternal things, and that the things that seem solid and important—house and car and *things*—are really the ephemeral things, the mortal things? No, of course not; like all but the crazily wise, we habitually looked at the world inside out, upside down and backwards. The nearness of death is a harsh but effective teacher. And it teaches also a second lesson, not to mind but to heart: the infinite preciousness of life. When every little thing becomes perhaps the last, every little thing becomes a big thing. Why must we wait till death is near to see this? Walter de la Mare advises "Look thy last on all things lovely every hour."

We thought, if this is the bad news we fear, we'll take her to Disneyland this summer, perhaps her last summer, certainly her last summer to travel semi-normally. Somehow we'll find the nonexistent money (death puts to death calculations). What a trip that would be: a thousand tearing, conflicting emotions, most of them without names. How raw the skin of our souls will be! A lot of psychic blood will be lost from our hearts; will any remain?

IV

The next image impressed on my memory is her mother camped out on the floor of her hospital room, not leaving her daughter's side day or night for weeks, patiently (she is not a patient person) enduring all her grouchiness, fussiness, and cussedness because it might be her last. Every word, every grouch is infinitely precious. Not because it is good but because it is hers. For love demands to be with her. Not even happiness is more precious to love than withness. "Better unhappy with her than happy without her" are the words of love.

It was easy and it was hard. The preciousness made it easy, necessary, inevitable. The pressure to act normal, not to break down, not to instill fear into her daughter, made it hard, very hard.

The mother lion guards her injured cub. She will not relax her vigil until all is well, though the whole world may sneer and call her unreasonable and overprotective. That is a judgment on the world, not on her. For she is enacting a mystery, a ritual that is larger and older than the world. Not only in her own name does she act, but also as representative for something transcendental, a mystery the human race has always felt and known until these times of uprootedness: Motherhood with a capital M, a metaphysical force of which human mothers are mere carriers. Her vocation speaks with authority—an absolute, and imperative, a divine revelation.

V

In her mother's arms outside the operating room, she fell asleep after a double dose of preliminary anaesthesia and double the expected time. We sang to her and spoke to her, as she drowsed off peacefully, of all the good things in her past and all the good things in her future. My voice cracked; when love and sorrow meet, the combustion cracks many things, including hearts and voices. I hope I didn't scare her. Finally, she slept and we gave her up to her surgeon, her fate, and her God.

Would this be the last time we would ever see her with hope? Would this be the last time we could see a twenty-year-old face behind her five-year-old face? Would this be the last time, even, we would see her alive? Operating tables aren't the safest places in the world, despite doctors' assurances.

When her head finally fell back and her eyelids drooped, it seemed almost as if she had died to us right then and there, although of course our minds told us it was only the anaesthesia working as it was supposed to work. And when the anaesthesiologist gently lifted her stone-still form from her mother's arms where she had fallen asleep so trustingly and almost contentedly, it was like an offering, a ritual sacrifice. They wheeled her away on a table, and it seemed as if the Angel of Death had accepted the sacrifice. When the table turned the corner into the operating room and we could follow it no longer, we turned our last corner. We had done all we could do. Our work was over, except to believe and to pray. Our physical part played out, we were played out. We let go, collapsed in each other's arms, and wept wordlessly.

One more scene etched unforgettably on the defenseless mind. The trusting child falling asleep—was it on the lap of Mother Life or Mother Death? The sleeping child—was it the sleep of healing or the sleep of dying? The taken-away child—was it just another step away from us, from her life, from her world, a step closer to death? The take-away scene looked like a little death.

Everything is a little death, a step toward the one end awaiting us all. But must it be now? *Now* makes a qualitative difference. Ivan Ilyitch found that out.

Is she so precious to Heaven that they can't wait for her? And what about us? Aren't we precious? Not too precious, I hope, not ready to be initiated into the greater mysteries of suffering yet. But she—the heavenly magnet seems to draw to itself the heavenly substance of her being, as if she were too heavenly to be on our dark earth for very long.

All we can do is to beg for the gift to be returned. We now know three things: whose gift it is, how infinitely precious it is, and what beggars we are.

VI

No one ever told me how incredibly similar grief and joy feel. Both are tired, numb, timeless, limbo feelings, a sheer state of *"be*-ing" with nothing added.

When we received the news that she was alive, the tumor was benign, and had been completely removed, we just grinned for eight straight hours. We stared smilingly at her beautiful living form. It was perfect, absolutely perfect. It looked like a turkey, with puffy eyes, shaved hair, and all sorts of tubes stuffed into her; yet never has anyone ever looked so beautiful to me. Nothing more was needed, nothing could be added; she was perfect. It was like having another baby, a new life.

How crazily close are the borders of heaven and hell on earth. From having lived on the rim of hell, thinking dead thoughts from a dead heart, I suddenly found myself closer to the rim of heaven than ever before. My child, whom I counted as dead, is alive again; the one who was lost is found. I shared the joy of the father of the prodigal son, of the shepherd finding the lost sheep, and perhaps even of God the Father at the resurrection of His Son. A remote but real beam of light from the heavenly sun.

In the light of life-and-death, how far away the near little things of the day become, and how near the far, great things of the night! The black light that death shines onto life is a clear light, an enlightening light. The country of the dead, from whose borders we have just returned, dispenses a great grace, a gift of vision, a third eye, a dimension of depth, a metaphysical X-ray. Death is the deepest place, and it enables love to speak its word *de profundis,* from the depths, from the deepest place of all. It adds a *basso profundo* to love's soprano, and all things work together in ultimate harmony.

Let us sing.